FALLING SHORT

FALLING SHORT

The Coming Retirement Crisis and
What to Do About It

By Charles D. Ellis, Alicia H. Munnell

AND

Andrew D. Eschtruth

OXFORD
UNIVERSITY PRESS

OXFORD
UNIVERSITY PRESS

Oxford University Press is a department of the University of
Oxford. It furthers the University's objective of excellence in research,
scholarship, and education by publishing worldwide.

Oxford   New York

Auckland   Cape Town   Dar es Salaam   Hong Kong   Karachi
Kuala Lumpur   Madrid   Melbourne   Mexico City   Nairobi
New Delhi   Shanghai   Taipei   Toronto

With offices in

Argentina   Austria   Brazil   Chile   Czech Republic   France   Greece
Guatemala   Hungary   Italy   Japan   Poland   Portugal   Singapore
South Korea   Switzerland   Thailand   Turkey   Ukraine   Vietnam

Oxford is a registered trademark of Oxford University Press
in the UK and certain other countries.

Published in the United States of America by
Oxford University Press
198 Madison Avenue, New York, NY 10016

© Oxford University Press 2014

Library of Congress Cataloging-in-Publication Data
Ellis, Charles D.
Falling short : the coming retirement crisis and what to do / by Charles D. Ellis, Alicia H.
Munnell, and Andrew D. Eschtruth.
pages cm
Includes bibliographical references and index.
ISBN 978–0–19–021889–8 (alk. paper)
1. Social security—United States.   2. Pensions—United States.   3. Retirement
income—United States.   I. Munnell, Alicia Haydock.   II. Eschtruth,
Andrew.   III. Title.
HD7125.E554 2015
331.25'20973—dc23
2014024776

3 5 7 9 8 6 4 2
Printed in the United States of America
on acid-free paper

CONTENTS

FALLING SHORT

[1]

INTRODUCTION

Just 30 years ago, most American workers were able to stop working in their early sixties and enjoy a long and comfortable retirement. This "golden age" of retirement security reflected the culmination of efforts that started more than a century ago when employers first set up pensions. Gradually, over decades, we built an effective system with Social Security and Medicare as the universal foundation and traditional pensions—where the employer was responsible for all the saving and investment decisions—providing a solid supplement for about half the workforce. The increasing provision of retirement support allowed people to retire earlier and earlier.

This brief golden age is now over. Because of economic and demographic developments, our retirement income systems are contracting just as our need for retirement income is growing. On the income side, Social Security is replacing less of our preretirement income; traditional defined benefit pension plans have been displaced by 401(k)s with modest balances; and employers are dropping retiree health benefits. On the needs side, longer lifespans, rising health care costs, and low interest rates all require a much bigger nest egg to maintain our standard of living. The result of all these changes is that millions of us will not have enough money for the comfortable retirement that our parents and grand-parents enjoyed.

If we do not recognize that we are veering off the road and take corrective action soon, millions of retirees will find that they are too old to return to work *and* have too little in savings—with no one to turn to for help. If we fail to recognize the problems and provide sensible solutions—now, when we can—history will judge us harshly. Millions of retirees will ask: "Why didn't anybody warn us?" Or, "You could see it coming! Why did you fail to do what was needed to be done to protect us?"

We hope this book—a little like Paul Revere's famous ride in 1775—will help raise the alarm and get government leaders, corporate executives, and individual workers thinking and talking about how to solve America's impending retirement crisis. We propose a number of specific and doable adjustments to get us back on the road and heading safely to our intended destination.

To provide a brief, but complete, guide to our retirement security challenge, this small book tackles three big questions: How did we get where we are? How bad is the problem? And what can we—as individuals and as a nation—do about it? The short answers are provided in this introductory chapter. But you will want to read the rest of the book for the full story.

At one level, our retirement problem is simple: we need more income, but we will get less from traditional sources. We need more because we are living longer while today's average retirement age is 64 for men and 62 for women.[1] As a result, the average man will spend 21 years in retirement, the average woman 23 years, and couples will face a significant probability of one member living into the nineties. We also need more income because out-of-pocket health costs are high and rising. And interest rates, which determine how much income we can draw from our nest eggs, have fallen to historic lows.

While we need more spendable income, we are now getting less from Social Security and employer pensions. Under current law, Social Security replacement rates are being gradually reduced as the so-called Full Retirement Age rises, Medicare premiums are taking a bigger bite of benefit checks, and more people are subject to taxes on their benefits. In addition, the shift to two-earner households is reducing replacement rates further. Moreover, Social Security faces a long-term deficit, so benefits could be cut even further to restore balance.

On the private employer side, traditional pensions are rapidly disappearing, replaced by 401(k) plans.[2] While these plans could be an effective way to save if structured appropriately, today they are clearly falling short. These plans shift all risks and responsibilities from the employer to the individual, and most of us are not well prepared for this burden. We make mistakes at each step along the way. The result is that most 401(k)s have only modest balances, which will produce far too little retirement income. For households nearing retirement with a 401(k), the typical total is only $111,000—including any assets that were rolled over into IRAs.[3] That $111,000 may seem like a lot to many, but it means less than $400 per month in retirement (adjusted annually for inflation) to supplement Social Security benefits that cover a shrinking share of our preretirement income. And those with a 401(k) are the lucky ones; half of today's private sector workers don't have any employer-sponsored retirement plan.

The one small bright spot in this gloomy picture is that many of us are saving through our house with each monthly mortgage payment, and we could tap this home equity in retirement to help pay the bills. But, even counting home equity, most of us do not have nearly enough. For example, to maintain their standard of living, a typical couple needs savings of 6 to 11 times their earnings (depending on when they retire) to supplement Social Security. But a typical household's current savings at retirement are much less than half that amount!

So what can we do—as individuals and as a nation? There are only three options. The first is to simply accept that we are going to be poor in retirement. The second is to save more while working, which means spending less today. The third is to work longer, which means fewer years in retirement. Those are our *only* options.

Every specific idea for solving the retirement income problem, whether it appears here or elsewhere, falls under one of these three options. For example, reducing Social Security benefits means living on less in retirement. Expanding participation in 401(k) plans means saving more. And explicitly recognizing that 70 is Social Security's *real* retirement age means encouraging people to work longer.

This book focuses on solving the retirement problem through a combination of working longer and saving more. (Living on a little less in retirement may, in the end, also be necessary, but it should not be our goal.) Achieving these aims will require a broad effort by individuals, by businesses, and by our government. Fortunately, we have both the ability and the financial infrastructure to meet the retirement challenge.

Let's start with working longer. Many of us are healthier and have less physically demanding jobs than our parents and grandparents. And we are living much longer. So stretching out our work lives is a sensible option. And the payoff is eye-popping! Individuals who delay receiving Social Security benefits from 62 to 70 increase their monthly benefits by a full 76 percent. Government could send a clear signal about the importance of working longer by vigorously promoting age 70 as the new 65. It should also consider raising Social Security's Earliest Eligibility Age from 62 to, say, 64.

(At the same time, we need to find a solution for those of us who simply cannot work longer due to health problems or outdated job skills.) Publicly encouraging longer work lives would signal to employers that older workers would be sticking around and, thus, would increase employers' willingness to hire, train, and promote them. For our part, as workers, we should do what we can to show our employers that we are hustling to keep up our technical skills.

On the saving front, we should first fix Social Security. Benefits are already shrinking relative to earnings, and additional cuts could cause steep drops in living standards and higher poverty. For that reason, reforms should lean much more toward higher revenues than lower benefits. And, to temper the need to raise payroll taxes, we should consider shifting the costs of the system's legacy burden to the personal income tax and perhaps investing part of trust fund assets in equities.

The next step is to boost our savings in 401(k)s through evolutionary improvements within the current structure. The key lever is to expand the use of the automatic 401(k), a model that is a proven success. Under this automatic approach—unless employees choose to opt out—they participate in the plan, their contributions rise each year until they reach a specified level, and their savings are invested in a balanced investment portfolio that can rely on index funds with low fees. If workers don't like one or more of the automatic provisions, they can opt out and make different decisions. But experience shows that most people are happy to stay where they are put. While the government currently *encourages* employers to adopt this auto-401(k) strategy, this approach has met with only limited success. We wish that all companies would adopt this successful model voluntarily but, given experience to date, we think the time may have come to make the automatic provisions *mandatory* and extend them to all employees, not just new hires.

As part of the evolutionary approach to boosting retirement saving, we need to solve the pension coverage gap for the half of workers without a 401(k) plan, perhaps by providing an "auto-IRA" at either the federal or state level or automatically enrolling all uncovered workers in President Obama's new "MyRA." Our retirement system will never be complete until all workers have an automatic saving option to supplement Social Security.

A key advantage to the evolutionary approach is its reliance on our existing programs and financial arrangements rather than trying to build a new system. However, some experts prefer starting over with a fresh approach. These "big bang" proposals, which feature universal accounts with low-cost investing and a reduced role for employers, are also discussed.

The final piece of the saving puzzle is the house. Most of us think of our house as a last-resort emergency fund—perhaps to pay for nursing home care—not as a source of day-to-day funds. And, if there's no emergency, we plan to pass it on to our kids. But the house is a big source of saving for most of us and often the *only* saving for those of us without a 401(k). Many of us will need to use our home equity to help pay the monthly bills in retirement, so we should consider tapping it through downsizing or taking a reverse mortgage.

That's it: work longer, fix Social Security, save more through 401(k)s, and consider using home equity. These steps are all doable, and they should all seem familiar. Working is something we've been doing all of our adult lives; we just have to plan to keep doing it longer than our parents did. Social Security has been, and should continue to be, the cornerstone of the system. Our 401(k)s can be made much better just by following the successful "automatic" model already in use. While the fixes for both Social Security and 401(k)s will require us to contribute more when we are working, lowering our spending somewhat now will give us a more realistic standard of living that is easier to maintain when we retire. And using our home equity to address important needs, such as renovations or college costs, is second nature for many of us. We just have to think of "retirement security" as an important need as well.

The bottom line is that a long retirement is expensive; it is difficult to prepare for because we are increasingly on our own; and, without making changes, we are not going to have nearly enough in savings. This discussion does not pit the old against the young, grandparents against their grandchildren. We all belong to families where we care about the generations ahead of and behind us. Rather the discussion is about what each of us should do when we are young and working so that we will have enough money when we stop working and about how the system could be better designed to help us in that effort. The world has changed, so we must adapt if we are going to have a decent retirement.

[2]

HOW DID WE GET HERE?

The story behind our current situation starts in the late nineteenth century with the emergence of retirement—a brief retirement—as a distinct part of life. From that point, the nation engaged in a century-long effort to ensure that people could retire with adequate income. This process proceeded in fits and starts, with many adjustments over time in response to unanticipated consequences or unexpected needs. By the late twentieth century, however, these collective efforts culminated in a brief "golden age," when many American workers retired with confidence in their financial security. But now, the promised benefits have become unsustainable and our retirement income system is coming up short, with many of us facing a serious mismatch between our retirement needs and retirement resources.

This chapter provides critical context for understanding why it is either not feasible or, in some cases, desirable to go back to the past. Instead the system needs to continue to evolve to meet the needs and challenges of today and those foreseeable over the coming decades.

THE EMERGENCE OF "RETIREMENT"

Retirement as a distinct stage of life is a fairly recent innovation.[1] Up to the end of the nineteenth century, most people worked for themselves as farmers or shopkeepers, and they worked as hard and as long as they could. In their prime, they worked 60 hours each week. As productive capacity declined with age, older people took on easier jobs or worked fewer hours, but they generally stopped working only when no longer able.[2] Well into the nineteenth century, about half of all 80-year-old men in America still worked.[3] At the end of life, workers—often already in poor health—had only a year or two of relative leisure.

Two developments—industrialization and urbanization—transformed the economics of aging in the nineteenth century. Industrialization transferred production from households to larger enterprises, creating an enormously productive economy. But industrialization also reduced the ability of older people to keep working, because they were no longer their own boss and employers were not interested in employing workers with deteriorating physical capacities. Therefore, at the end of the nineteenth century, employment among men 65 and over began to decline sharply (see figure 2.1).[4]

Industrialization also separated earning a living from acquiring income-producing property. In the preindustrial era, family farms were natural ways to accumulate wealth, and many older workers were able to retire on incomes from selling or leasing those assets.[5] In contrast, industrial workers did not own the factories, so to accumulate wealth they needed to set aside part of their earnings and invest. Few did. Successful saving and investing requires foresight, discipline, and skill. And, at the beginning of the industrialization process, when retirement was just emerging as a distinct stage of life, workers had no role models to copy. Retirement saving did not seem necessary because penalties for not saving were not obvious.

At the same time that workers were losing family farms as a natural way of accumulating wealth, demographic changes made

Figure 2.1. Men Retired Earlier and Earlier from the 1880s to the 1980s
Workforce Participation Rates of Men, by Age Group, 1880–2012

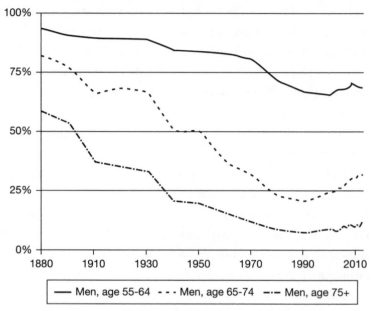

Source: University of Minnesota, Integrated Public Use Microdata Series (1880–2012).

for longer retirements with less family support. Urbanization concentrated the population in the large labor and product markets. Medical and public health advances in these urban areas increased life expectancies, so older people faced a longer period of life without income from work. At the same time, families in the city found children less advantageous than on the farm, so the size of families declined. As a result, aged parents had fewer children to support them when they could no longer earn a living.

Fortunately, an unexpected and substantial stream of income for the elderly appeared toward the end of the nineteenth century in the form of old-age pensions for the large number of Union Army Civil War veterans who had become disabled. But many older veterans who did not qualify for these pensions became charity cases. In response, the federal government expanded Civil War pensions to include all veterans, allowing more men to retire with dignity.[6]

But soon those eligible for the Civil War pensions began to die off, and new generations of elderly had no obvious source of retirement income.[7] Yet the percentage of the older population at work continued to decline. Without either work or savings, the relative economic status of the aged fell sharply. In response to both the needs of the growing number of distressed older workers and the new industrialists, large employers and government created retirement programs.

BEGINNING A RETIREMENT INCOME SYSTEM: 1900–1939

The private sector led the way with the establishment of pensions for employees, and the federal government followed with the enactment of Social Security in 1935.[8]

Establishment of Corporate and Union Pensions

The large, prosperous, and heavily regulated transportation industry, which employed many workers in hazardous jobs, pioneered the establishment of private plans.[9] Pensions helped develop career employees and managers, to whom large employers increasingly delegated authority. Pensions paid a comfortable benefit—pegged to salary and years of service—to those white-collar workers who remained to the specified retirement age. Workers who left early typically got only a return of their own contributions. Pensions provided a strong incentive to remain with the company and to rise through the ranks.

Pensions also proved valuable in shaping relationships with blue-collar workers. Organizations in industries such as railroads, urban transit, and manufacturing employed very large numbers of blue-collar workers to operate their capital-intensive operations. These employers typically paid above-market wages to attract better workers, win their loyalty, and fend off unions. But beyond a certain point, employers found it more effective to provide "industrial insurance" rather than ever-higher wages. This insurance protected workers and their families against the loss of earnings due to accident, death, illness, or old age.

At the same time, many large employers saw their offices, machine shops, and locomotives increasingly staffed by older workers whose productivity had clearly declined. So beginning at the turn of the century in the United States, large employers began to mandate retirement at a specified age. To remove older workers without damaging relations with the rest of the workforce, or the public at large, they retired these workers with pensions.

While large industrial employers were establishing pension plans, a small number of trade unions were instituting their own schemes for retirement benefits. Mutual benefit societies for survivor, sickness, and disability were traditional among unions, but the first union old-age plan (established by the Granite Cutters) did not appear until 1905.[10]

Both the industrial and union pensions were defined benefit plans, which pay retirement benefits in the form of a lifetime annuity. The annuity might be a dollar amount per month or a percentage of final salary, for each year of service. The employer finances these benefits by making pretax contributions into a pension fund; employees typically do not contribute. The employer holds the assets in trust, directs the investments, assumes the investment risk, and bears the mortality risk of providing lifelong benefits.

The Great Depression had a profound effect on both corporate and union plans. Of particular note, the railroad industry was operating in the red and did not have pension reserves to help pay benefits. Because so many people were involved in this major industry, Congress nationalized these plans. Many employees covered by other corporate and union plans were not so fortunate; these workers lost some or all of their anticipated benefits.

Social Security

The Depression not only depleted most pension plans, it also undermined Americans' confidence in the historic tradition of self-reliance and the virtue of individual thrift. By 1933, about 25 percent of the workforce—nearly 13 million people—were out of work, and the lifetime savings of many were gone. The Social Security Act of 1935 was both a response to the widespread unemployment and poverty created by the Great Depression *and* an effort to provide a permanent solution to the long-standing problem of economic insecurity for older Americans.[11]

The Old-Age Insurance portion of the 1935 Social Security Act bore a much stronger resemblance to a private insurance plan than to the system we know today. It provided only retirement benefits and only to the worker. The legislation called for the accumulation of a trust fund and stressed the principle of a fair return.[12] The 1939 Amendments, however, fundamentally changed the nature of the program by adding two new types of benefits: payments to the spouse and minor children of a retired worker (dependent benefits) and payments to the spouse and minor children of a worker who dies (survivor benefits). These changes transformed Social Security from an insurance plan for individual workers into a family-based economic security program and significantly weakened the link between lifetime contributions and benefits.

Moreover, the legislation accelerated the payment of benefits so individuals who had worked only a few years under the system were entitled to receive full benefits. This decision shifted the financing model from a funded system to pay-as-you-go, with big implications for the cost of Social Security benefits today. If earlier cohorts had received only the benefits that could have been financed by their contributions plus interest, trust fund assets and interest earnings would be much larger today and the required tax on our current earnings much lower.

The Depression represented a transitional stage for the US retirement income system. The nation entered World War II with the Social Security legislation enacted, but the program still in its infancy, and with employer pensions established as a standard feature of US personnel systems, but facing significant financial challenges.

EXPANDING THE PROGRAMS: 1949–1979

Although World War II consumed many resources that might have been directed toward improved provisions for old age, wartime wage controls and the postwar economic expansion provided the basis for reinvigorating both corporate and union pensions and the Social Security program. This period also included the enactment of Medicare and Medicaid.

Rebuilding the Pension System

Despite the diversion of resources, wartime wage controls had provided some support for the expansion of private plans. The War Labor Board, which had set legal limitations on cash wages to keep a lid on inflation, permitted employers to bid for workers by offering attractive fringe benefits. Pension benefits cost firms little in view of the wartime excess profits tax and employers' ability to deduct pension contributions (see box 2.1 for a description of tax provisions). As a result, pensions increased as a share of total compensation.

In the immediate postwar period, employees focused on cash wages to recover ground lost during wartime wage stabilization. But by 1949, pension benefits became a major issue in labor negotiations because of increased employer resistance to further wage hikes, a weak economy, and the obvious inadequacy of Social Security benefits. Labor's drive for pension benefits was aided when the Supreme Court confirmed that employers had a legal obligation to negotiate the terms of pension plans.[13] The United Steelworkers and the United Automobile Workers then launched successful drives for pension benefits. Other unions soon followed.

The main expansion of today's private pension system occurred between 1950 and 1960 (see figure 2.2). Private pension coverage grew rapidly in both unionized and nonunionized industries. The Korean War further stimulated the pension movement as employers once again competed for workers in the face of wage and salary controls and excess profits taxes. The mid-1950s also marked substantial collective bargaining gains in multiemployer plans and in state and municipal government plans.

The number of covered workers continued to grow in the 1960s, primarily through expansion of employment in firms that already had pension plans as opposed to the establishment of new

Box 2.1 tax incentives for retirement saving

Saving for retirement is a tax-advantaged activity. The conventional rationale for providing such treatment is that, without it, very little retirement saving would occur, which would put pressure on government means-tested programs for retirees. Whether our current tax incentives are efficient or optimal is an open question, which is covered later.

The specific tax incentives are as follows. Employers and individuals take an immediate deduction for contributions to retirement plans and participants pay no tax on investment returns until benefits are paid out in retirement.[14] (If saving were done outside the plan, individuals would first be required to pay tax on their earnings and then on the returns from the portion of those earnings invested.) The favorable tax treatment significantly reduces the lifetime taxes of those who receive part of their compensation in contributions to retirement plans relative to those who receive all their earnings in cash wages.[15] The favorable treatment accorded retirement plans costs the Treasury the difference between the present value of revenue foregone and the present value of future taxes each year. The 2012 cost to the Treasury from retirement plans is estimated at $164 billion.[16] To put this figure in some context, it amounts to 12 percent of federal income tax revenues or roughly the amount spent on US military personnel.[17]

plans. Pension coverage continued to expand slightly until the end of the 1970s, reaching about half of the private sector workforce—where it remains today.

The expansion of pension coverage—and the tax-favored status of the plans—heightened congressional interest in ensuring that the plans provided retirement benefits to the rank and file as well as to highly compensated employees. It became clear that some employers imposed such stringent vesting and participation standards that many rank-and-file workers reached retirement age only to discover that they failed to qualify for a pension because of a layoff, a merger, or a bankruptcy. The fate of workers in the South Bend, Indiana, plant closed by Studebaker in 1963 is the best-known example of substantial benefit losses due to the bankruptcy of an employer. After more

Figure 2.2. Employer Pension Coverage Rose until the 1970s
Percentage of US Private Sector Workers Covered by Employer Plans, 1880–2012

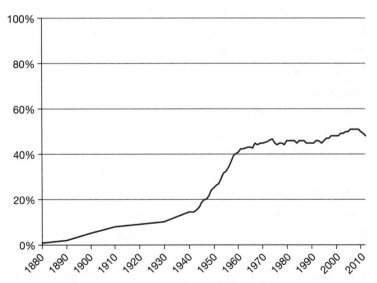

Sources: Skolnik (1976); US Department of Labor (1999); US Bureau of Labor Statistics, National Compensation Survey (1999–2012); and authors' estimates.

than 10 years of hearings and prolonged debate, Congress passed ERISA—the Employee Retirement Income Security Act—in 1974. ERISA's principal objective is to see that a greater proportion of covered workers earn pension credits during their working years and receive pension benefits in retirement. ERISA also established the Pension Benefit Guaranty Corporation, a mandatory insurance program to protect workers' benefits if an employer terminates a plan with inadequate assets.

Expanding Social Security

The period between 1949 and 1979 also witnessed an enormous expansion of the Social Security program. By their nature, pension systems mature slowly because, when they start, those already retired are not included. So, in 1950—15 years after the initial legislation—only about 25 percent of retirees were protected by Social Security.[18] Moreover, by design, some had been excluded from the program. This situation led to Social Security amendments in 1950 and 1954, which substantially expanded coverage to include farm and domestic workers and the self-employed, except those in law (included in 1956) and medicine (included in 1965). By the mid-1960s, coverage was virtually complete, except for about 30 percent of state and local government workers who are still uncovered today.[19] As Social Security broadened coverage, it also began allowing more flexibility in the age at which people could claim benefits (see box 2.2).

In addition to the need for broader coverage, the value of Social Security benefits had been severely eroded. As a result of the "double whammy" of the postwar surge in wages *and* inflation, benefits for new retirees were as little as 15 percent of preretirement earnings. The 1950 legislation increased benefits significantly, raising the replacement rate—benefits as a percent of preretirement earnings—to about 28 percent. The benefit formula was then changed seven times between 1950 and 1970 to keep the replacement rate at about 28 percent (see figure 2.3). Subsequent legislation in 1970 and 1971 raised the replacement rate to about 35 percent.

Box 2.2 social security's retirement age

Social Security was designed to replace income once people could no longer work. In the 1930s, the retirement age was set at 65, which coincided with the age used by many private and public pension plans. In the late 1950s and early 1960s, Congress changed the law to enable workers to claim benefits as early as 62. But benefits claimed before 65 were actuarially reduced, so that those who claimed at 62 and those who claimed at 65 could expect to receive about the same total amount in benefits over their lifetimes.

In the early 1970s, Congress introduced the Delayed Retirement Credit, which increased monthly benefits for those who claimed after the "Full Retirement Age," then 65. That credit was modest at first but, after several increases, now fully compensates for delayed claiming. As a result, lifetime benefits are roughly equal for any claiming age between 62 and 70, and the highest monthly benefits are available at 70.

In 2014, the relevant retirement ages were as follows:

62: Earliest possible claiming age (Earliest Eligibility Age).

66: Technical age used for determining base benefit (Full Retirement Age).

70: Age at which maximum monthly benefits are available.

Figure 2.3. Social Security Became More Generous during Postwar Economic Boom

Social Security Replacement Rate for Medium Earner Retiring at Age 65, 1940–2013

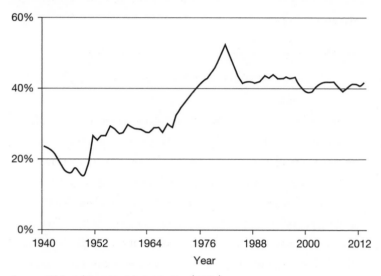

Source: US Social Security Administration (2013c).

In 1972, legislation further increased benefits and introduced automatic adjustments in the benefit calculation to stabilize the initial replacement rate and to automatically adjust benefits after retirement for increases in the Consumer Price Index.[20] Since 1977, the Social Security benefit calculation has been on auto-pilot with a replacement rate of about 40 percent for the average earner—the level intended in 1972.[21]

The Introduction of Medicare and Medicaid

In 1965, Congress enacted Medicare, a health insurance program for the elderly and disabled, and Medicaid, a means-tested healthcare program for those with low income and few assets. Medicare has three components: hospital insurance (also known as Part A), supplementary medical insurance (Part B), and the prescription drug program (Part D, introduced in 2006). Under Part A, workers and their employers contribute payroll taxes over their work lives and are entitled to payments to cover the cost of hospital care once they reach age 65. Parts B and D, which cover physician services and drugs respectively, are financed by both general revenues and current premiums. Individuals are responsible for deductibles and copayments, and Medicare does not cover more than temporary long-term care, so the elderly needing long-term coverage must make substantial out-of-pocket payments. Nevertheless, Medicare greatly enhanced the financial security and health of older Americans. Medicaid also helps the elderly because it pays for nursing home care for those who meet very strict income and asset tests. Medicaid covers almost 40 percent of all nursing home expenditures, as well as about 15 percent of home healthcare outlays.[22]

In short, the period from 1949 to 1979 saw the expansion of Social Security, the introduction of Medicare and Medicaid, *and* the maturation of the private sector's defined benefit pension system, buttressed by generous tax subsidies. Nearly a century after the emergence of retirement as a distinct period of life, America had created a system to ensure that people had the income and healthcare they would need in retirement.

THE GOLDEN AGE: 1980–2000

Those who retired in the 1980s and 1990s enjoyed a "golden age" in the history of US retirement programs. During this period, pension coverage remained at about half of private sector workers (see figure 2.2), and most people retiring with coverage had a traditional defined benefit pension plan. The defined benefit system was not perfect—only a fraction of the workforce was covered, mobile employees forfeited benefits, and benefits were not adjusted for inflation. But for those with coverage, the employer took care of retirement planning and provided an income for life. Most of those with defined benefit pension coverage also enjoyed retiree health insurance provided by their employer.

During the 1980s and 1990s, Social Security benefits replaced about 40 percent of preretirement income for the average worker, the age for full benefits was 65, and many couples still qualified for substantial spousal benefits. Medicare covered most healthcare spending; for the typical beneficiary in 1997, out-of-pocket health costs were only 12 percent of income.[23]

Confirmation of the golden age comes from assessments of participants in the *Health and Retirement Study*, a national longitudinal survey that began in 1992 with participants reinterviewed every two years. The survey asks, "All in all, would you say that your retirement has turned out to be very satisfying, moderately satisfying or not at all satisfying?" In the 1990s, among those who considered themselves completely retired, 61 percent said that their retirement was very satisfying. After the turn of the century, that figure began to decline, and by 2012 had dropped to 51 percent.[24] The percentage finding retirement very satisfying is likely to decline even further as the provisions of the golden age apply to fewer and fewer retirees.

RETRENCHMENT AFTER 2000

The golden age ended around the turn of the century. While private pension coverage remained roughly constant, fewer and fewer workers participated in defined benefit plans, employers backed away from retiree health insurance, and the age for "full" Social Security benefits began to increase gradually from 65 to 67.

The Shift from Defined Benefit to 401(k) Plans

The shift in the nature of plans offered by private sector employers reflected pressures on sponsors of defined benefit plans and the advent in the early 1980s of the 401(k) plan.

Defined Benefit Plans under Pressure

ERISA was designed to preserve benefits for employees covered by private sector defined benefit plans, but the original legislation and subsequent amendments during the 1980s also increased regulatory burdens and costs. Then, major economic shocks hit key U.S. industries—specifically, steel and airlines—whose pension plans had large unfunded liabilities. These shocks led to large pension insolvencies, major deficits at the government insurance fund, and the imposition of tougher funding requirements, primarily on sponsors of weak defined benefit plans. Congress also imposed an excise tax on employers who reclaim the excess assets of terminated defined benefit plans.

These regulatory pressures coincided with other costly developments: workers were living longer, which made lifetime benefits increasingly expensive, and inflation declined, which raised the real cost of un-indexed lifetime payments. Moreover, in less-than-fully-funded plans, a dramatic increase in the number of retirees required large contributions relative to the size of the company. Finally, significant swings in equity prices produced unpredictable mandatory pension contributions in large maturing plans that, with new accounting regulations, affected reported company earnings.

In addition to regulatory and cost pressures, other changes—globalization, sharp increases in workers' education, increasingly technical production, and employment of married women—made defined benefit plans less attractive. First, these changes diminished the power of unions, a major factor in the postwar expansion of employer plans. Second, these changes undermined the financial stability of large corporate employers, making the assumption of long-term pension obligations a more risky undertaking. Finally, the changing labor force—more female, educated, and young—reduced the appeal of life-long careers, especially for the higher-paid workers that employer retirement plans primarily serve. As a result, employers started to move away from defined benefit plans as a tool of personnel management. Virtually no new company of any size established a defined benefit plan.[25]

Although employers with existing defined benefit plans enjoyed smooth sailing during the 1990s as the stock market boom increased plan assets, trouble emerged at the turn of the century. The slump in the equities markets (producing a drop in the value of pension fund *assets*) and the decline in interest rates (producing a sharp rise in the present value of future plan *obligations*) required employers to nearly triple their annual pension contributions.[26] These developments had a dramatic effect on the finances of employers and intensified their interest in getting away from defined benefit commitments. Companies began closing defined benefit plans to new entrants or ending pension accruals for current as well as future employees.[27] Prior to 2000 it was very unusual for a company to close its defined benefit plan and institute a defined contribution plan, but after 2000 this change became routine.

The Advent of 401(k) Plans

As employers moved away from defined benefit plans, a new form of defined contribution plan emerged—the 401(k).[28] With a 401(k), the employee, and most often the employer, contributes a percentage of the employee's earnings into a retirement savings account.[29] These contributions are invested, generally at the direction of the employee, mostly in mutual funds of stocks and bonds. Employees do not pay taxes on 401(k) contributions or investment earnings over the course of their employment. When they retire, the balance in the account determines the retirement benefit. While employers sometimes offer different options for withdrawing the money, most employees take their balance as a lump-sum amount and roll it over into an IRA.[30] They then pay taxes on the amounts withdrawn from the IRA.

The 401(k) appealed to both employees and employers. Employees could make tax-deductible contributions and gained control of their retirement planning. Young, mobile workers could easily take their 401(k) accumulations with them as they moved from job to job. Rapidly rising account balances—during the long bull market of the 1980s and 1990s—convinced many people that they were good investors. From the employer's perspective, 401(k) plans offered a form of pension that workers appreciated greatly and eliminated the long-term risk to employers of funding lifetime retirement benefits and the near-term risk of large fluctuations in their required pension contributions. The cost of a 401(k) plan was highly predictable—increasingly important during the 1980s—and evolving computer and communications technology made administering the numerous individual accounts in a 401(k) plan much easier. Finally, 401(k)s shifted the cost of investment management—in the form of mutual fund fees—from employers to employees.

As a result of the adoption of 401(k)s by new companies, the decline in employment in industries with defined benefit plans, the termination of these plans in distressed industries, and more recently, the freezing of these plans even by healthy companies, the nature of employer-sponsored pension coverage has changed dramatically. While, in the early 1980s, the vast majority of workers who were lucky enough to have an employer-sponsored plan were covered by a defined benefit plan, by the turn of the century most covered workers had a 401(k) as their primary or only plan (see figure 2.4).

The unique structure of the 401(k) can be attributed to the fact that, when 401(k) plans began to spread rapidly in the 1980s, they were viewed mainly as supplements to employer-funded defined benefit pension and profit-sharing plans. Since participants were presumed to have their basic retirement income needs covered, they were given substantial discretion over key 401(k) choices, including whether to participate, how much to contribute, how to invest, what to do when changing jobs, and when and in what form to withdraw funds during retirement. Today, 401(k)s still operate largely under these same rules even though they are now the primary plan for most workers. As a consequence, workers have almost complete discretion over investment and savings choices, bear all the market risks, and face the risk of either overspending and outliving their retirement savings or spending too cautiously and consuming too little. On the accumulation side, one bright spot is the recent move by some plans to adopt automatic features in their 401(k)s that make default choices for individuals unless they opt out. At this point, though, these features cover only a minority of workers. And, at retirement, participants—who generally do not use their 401(k) balance to buy an annuity—are still

Figure 2.4. Employer Plans Have Shifted to 401(k)s
Workers with Pension Coverage by Type of Plan, 1983, 1992, 2001, and 2013

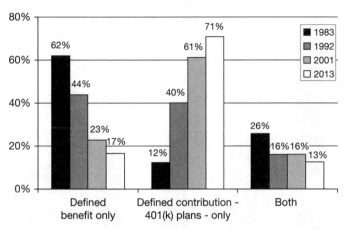

Source: Authors' calculations based on US Board of Governors of the Federal Reserve System, Survey of Consumer Finances (1983, 1992, 2001, and 2013).

on their own when it comes to deciding how to draw down their nest egg.

Employers Withdraw from Retiree Health Insurance

In addition to moving away from providing guaranteed retirement income, employers have also cut back on postretirement healthcare. Between 1988 and 2013, the share of large firms offering these benefits dropped sharply from 66 percent to 28 percent (see figure 2.5). In addition, the generosity of benefits was also reduced; employers required increased retiree contributions to insurance premiums, more coinsurance or copayments, larger deductibles, and higher out-of-pocket

Figure 2.5. Firms Have Cut Back on Retiree Health Coverage

Percentage of Large Employers Offering Retiree Health Benefits, 1988–2013

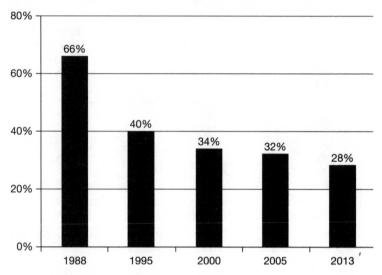

Source: Health Research & Educational Trust (2013).

limits.[31] And many of those companies still providing postretirement health benefits have terminated such benefits for new retirees. Thus, many workers will need to save more now than in the past to cover healthcare costs previously borne by their employers.

Retrenchment of Social Security

Soon after Social Security's expansion in the 1970s, it became clear that the decline in the birth rate was most likely permanent (see figure 2.6). Stable population growth combined with continued increases in life expectancy meant that the cost of the pay-as-you-go program would rise substantially. A short-term funding crisis in the early 1980s forced the government to act on

Figure 2.6 .Falling Birth Rates Are a Major Driver of an Aging Society
Fertility Rates in the United States, 1800–2080

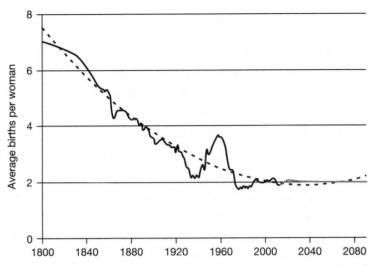

Sources: Coale and Zelnick (1963); Bell (1997); US Social Security Administration (2013d).

Social Security's finances. The National Commission on Social Security Reform, headed by Alan Greenspan, presented a series of reforms—involving both revenue increases and benefit cuts—that enabled the system to pay immediate benefits and restored solvency over the program's 75-year horizon. The major benefit cut in the 1983 reform package was the gradual extension beginning in 2000 of the "Full Retirement Age" from 65 to 67. As discussed in the next chapter, this change means that the Social Security replacement rate for the typical worker at age 65 will drop from about 40 percent to 36 percent by 2030.

Despite the 1983 changes, a deficit appeared almost immediately and increased sharply in the early 1990s. The main reason for this deficit was the changing 75-year valuation period. Each year the trustees of the Social Security program report to

Congress their estimates of revenues and costs over the next 75 years.[32] The 1983 report looked at the system's finances over the period 1983–2057, while the projection period for the 1984 report was 1984–2058. The single year added to the projection period (2058) showed a large deficit due to the high costs associated with the aging of the population, while the year deleted (1983) had had a slight surplus because of the recently enacted legislation. Each time the valuation period moved out one year, it picked up another year with a large deficit and dropped a year of surplus. The shift in the valuation period accounts for about two-thirds of the 2014 deficit.

Social Security can pay full benefits through 2033.[33] Thereafter, payroll taxes cover only about 75 percent of commitments. The financing shortfall means that the American people will have to choose either an increase in taxes, a further reduction in benefits, or a combination of the two.[34]

Medicare Under Pressure

Medicare spending has grown steadily in absolute dollars, as a share of the federal budget, and as a share of national output. The increase in Medicare costs reflects rising healthcare costs generally, caused primarily by the introduction of new technologies and the wider use of existing ones. The aging of the population will also increase Medicare costs, but this effect is small compared to the general rise in healthcare costs. With the growth in healthcare costs, out-of-pocket spending has increased rapidly to about 20 percent of beneficiaries' income.[35]

Although future growth in Medicare spending is projected to slow, these projections assume large cuts in physician fees that are scheduled under current law. If these cuts are blocked, as they have been numerous times in the past, Medicare spending will exceed projections.[36] Implementation of the Patient Protection and Affordable Care Act of 2010 will affect both Medicare spending and policy, but the net reduction in costs projected over the period 2010–19 is relatively modest. The most recent Trustees Report shows that the Medicare Part A (hospital insurance) trust fund will be exhausted in 2030, and that Medicare Parts B and D will require a substantial increase in participant premiums and taxes to finance current benefits.[37]

Proposals abound to reduce Medicare spending. Most of the proposals—raise the eligibility age to 67, increase Part B premiums to 35 percent of program costs, further raise Part B premiums for upper-income beneficiaries, or raise copayments and deductibles—simply shift costs to the individual participants. While more dramatic changes, such as providing individuals with a fixed dollar amount to purchase private insurance, are advertised as a way to control healthcare costs, they would leave older Americans with an increased financial burden.[38] Unless we can get healthcare spending under control, the government is likely to pull back on its commitment to cover these costs.

CONCLUSION

In response to the emergence at the end of the nineteenth century of retirement as a distinct part of life, America established public and private systems to support retirees. We did a good job. Many people retiring in the 1980s and 1990s retired comfortably. But the programs that supported that comfortable retirement soon confronted economic and demographic changes that made them unsustainable.

People who say America has a strong retirement system today are looking backward. We cannot go back to the golden age. Social Security is now mature and expensive; people are paying the full cost of their benefits and are also paying for the fact that we paid out benefits to the first cohort of retirees. In the private sector, defined benefit plans have largely disappeared; increasingly people will have to rely only on defined contribution 401(k) plans. Employers are out of the retiree healthcare business, and Medicare is under pressure. If we continue to retire in our early sixties, we will not have enough saved to support our standard of living for 20 or more years of retirement. So we must adjust in one way or another—accept lower living standards once we stop working, save more while working, and/or work longer. The next chapter explores the magnitude of the challenge we face.

[3]

HOW BIG IS THE PROBLEM?

America's retirement problem is very big and getting bigger every year. Baby boomers—and those who follow—will retire in a much different situation than their parents. They will need to finance their consumption for a longer time and will receive less retirement support from both Social Security and employer-sponsored plans.

This chapter describes what makes saving for retirement so challenging for individuals and then summarizes what we can expect from Social Security and 401(k) plans. The chapter begins by defining a reasonable goal for retirement saving—maintaining our standard of living in retirement—and then provides a yardstick—the "replacement rate"—to measure how close we are to achieving that goal. The replacement rate determines how much income we need each year; the expected years in retirement then determine the size of the savings required to produce that annual income. The required savings are much larger than our actual savings. So our annual income in retirement will fall short—far short—of maintaining our standard of living.

THE GOAL

Economists' life cycle model suggests that people maximize their well-being by smoothing consumption over their lifespan.[1] In practical terms, most of us would agree that maintaining our pre-retirement lifestyle after we stop working has great appeal: to stay in the same house surrounded by familiar objects, in a neighborhood where we have friends and know the shopkeepers, and to be able to go to the movies, eat out occasionally, visit our grandchildren, and maybe even travel a little.

To do all those things requires income, but not quite as much income as before retirement. One big difference before and after retirement is the extent to which income is taxed. When working, earnings are subject to both Social Security and Medicare payroll taxes and to federal personal income taxes. After retirement, we no longer pay payroll taxes, and we pay lower federal income taxes because only a portion of Social Security benefits is taxable. Another difference is that, as retirees, we require less income because we no longer need to save for retirement. And work-related expenses, such as clothing and transportation, are no longer necessary. Finally, many households pay off their mortgage before they retire (though fewer do so now than in the past). For all these reasons, a greater share of our income in retirement is available for consumption.

That leads us to the important yardstick of the replacement rate—the ratio of retirement income to preretirement income.[2] The notion is that some target replacement rate, which is derived from a consumption smoothing model, allows us to maintain our lifestyles; anything less, we fall short. For simplicity, the following discussion assumes that the average household needs a 75 percent replacement rate. The question then becomes: "How close do we come to the 75 percent rate?" The answer, for most of us, is not nearly close enough![3]

THE NEED FOR RETIREMENT INCOME

The crux of the retirement crisis is that a substantial gap has opened up between the resources we need for a secure retirement and the income we can currently expect from our nation's retirement programs: Social Security and 401(k) plans. Let's look first at the needs side and then see what is happening on the income side.

Increasing Years in Retirement

The key to the needs side is our increasing retirement span: we need to support ourselves—without earnings from work—for many more years than in the past. This growing retirement period substantially increases the savings we need to reach our target replacement rates.

The length of retirement depends on two factors: (1) the age at which we retire; and (2) how long we live after retirement. For many years, from the 1880s to the mid-1980s, the average retirement age was declining. This long-run trend toward earlier retirements began with Civil War pensions and continued with the enactment of Social Security and the expansion of employer pensions. The downward trend got a further boost from the introduction of Medicare in 1965, the sharp increase in Social Security benefits in 1972, and the spread of early retirement benefits in pension plans (see the gray line in figure 3.1).

Figure 3.1. Retirements Have Gotten Longer
Average Years in Retirement, 1960–2050

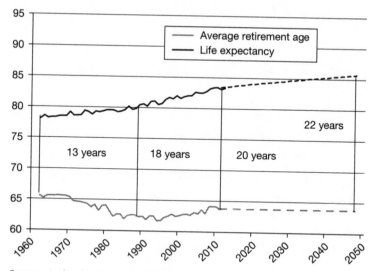

Sources: Authors' estimates from US Census Bureau, *Current Population Survey* (1962–2012); US Social Security Administration (2013b).

The downward trend stopped in the mid-1980s. Since then, the average retirement age for men has increased by two years (from 62 to 64).[4] This turnaround is attributed to many factors: the rise in Social Security's Delayed Retirement Credit (which increases benefits for those who retire later), the movement away from traditional defined benefit plans with their early retirement incentives, a better educated workforce with less physically demanding jobs, and the desire in the face of rising healthcare costs to maintain employer health coverage until reaching Medicare eligibility at 65.[5] An open question is whether these factors will continue to lead to later retirement ages or whether they have largely played out. Some argue that changes in educational attainment, which played a major role and have now plateaued, are unlikely to provide any further impetus.[6] In addition, the Affordable Care Act—by expanding access to nongroup health insurance—may reduce "job lock" and enable older workers to leave the labor force earlier than they would have otherwise (see box 3.1).

Meanwhile, life expectancy at 65 has been rising steadily for both men and women. Between 1960 and 2020, the average increase will be more than six years for men and more than four years for women (see table 3.1). Note that if the average life

---

Box 3.1 potential impact of the affordable care act
on work and retirement decisions

The Congressional Budget Office (CBO) estimates that the Affordable Care Act could reduce hours worked by 1.5 to 2.0 percent during 2017–2024.[7] Much of the CBO analysis relates to decisions by prime-age workers, but near-retirees could be affected as well. Traditionally, because of the high cost of health insurance, older workers have had an incentive to keep working to maintain their employer insurance until they become eligible for Medicare at age 65. Several of the Act's provisions—particularly the prohibition on denying coverage to individuals with preexisting conditions and restrictions on higher premiums due to age—reduce the cost of health insurance for older workers outside of the workplace. This access to affordable health insurance will reduce "job lock" and allow earlier retirement. Retiring earlier could improve the welfare of older individuals who were working simply to maintain their health insurance, but it raises the question whether their retirement security could be diminished.

Table 3.1 Life Expectancy at Age 65 Is Rising

	Men	Women
1960	13.2	17.4
1980	14.7	18.8
2000	17.6	20.3
2020	19.7	21.9

Source: US Social Security Administration (2013b).

expectancy at 65 is 20 years, the expectation is that one in four people will live for 25 years and one in five more than 30 years. So the potential for a very long life is high.

Figure 3.1 brings together the retirement-age and life-expectancy sides of the equation to show the expected years in retirement for the average male—now nearly 20 years. And the span will rise as life expectancy increases, unless people start retiring later. Averages, however, do not tell the whole story. First, as noted above, one-quarter of the population—generally the better educated and wealthier—will live at least five years longer than average. Second, most people retire as a couple, and a couple retiring today faces a 50 percent chance of at least one member living to 92. Thus, many people must plan on supporting themselves for a very long time after they stop working.

Rising Healthcare Costs

In addition to preparing for much longer retirements, we need to save more to cover the increasing costs of healthcare in retirement.

The major healthcare expenses, as noted in chapter 2, include Medicare premiums, copayments for Medicare-covered services, and the cost of services that are not covered by Medicare. In 2012, Medicare annual out-of-pocket expenses averaged $7,500 for a couple. In addition, retirees are responsible for all expenses not covered by Medicare, such as dental care, eyeglasses, and hearing aids. Moreover, medical costs have generally been rising rapidly. For example, out-of-pocket expenditures for Medicare Part B premiums and copayments have risen from 6.8 percent of the average Social Security benefit in 1980 to 16.5 percent today and are projected to reach 18.9 percent in 2030.[8] Estimates are that the average couple at age 65 faces about $200,000 in out-of-pocket and noncovered medical expenses during their retirement years.[9] One way to manage these health cost risks is to purchase insurance, such as a Medi-gap policy, but premiums must cover average costs and be paid out of current income. Long-term care also looms as an additional expense. Given rising healthcare costs, the 75 percent replacement rate target may, if anything, be on the low side of what we will need to maintain our standard of living.

Low Returns

In addition to needing more savings to support longer retirements and rapidly rising costs of medical care, retirees face lower rates of return on their investments than in the past. In particular, real interest rates have fallen dramatically from the record high rates of the late 1970s and early 1980s (see figure 3.2). Therefore, to reach the income replacement rate target, we will need more savings than in the past—much more.

Figure 3.2. Interest Rates Have Fallen to Historic Lows
Real Interest Rate, 1982–2013

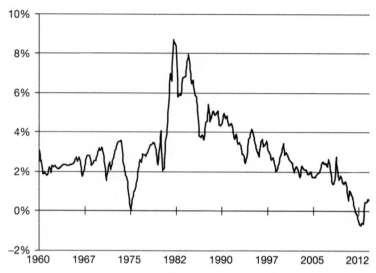

Sources: US Board of Governors of the Federal Reserve System (2013a); Haubrich, Pennacchi, and Ritchken (2011); and unpublished estimates from Richard Kopcke.

Need for Social Security and 401(k) Balances

If retirement ages stay at their current levels, Americans face an enormous saving challenge. (As discussed later, working longer is one of the key levers to solving the retirement income crisis.) Realistically, the only effective way to save more is through organized savings programs, because we just do not save on our own. In 2013, the average American household approaching retirement (age 55–64) held only $12,500 in financial assets outside of retirement plans. (These balances were depressed by the financial crisis, but even at the peak of the boom in 2007 financial assets for this group amounted to only $29,600.)[10]

The one place where many households build up resources that could be used in retirement is the house. Typically, people purchase homes early in their lives, financing them with a substantial mortgage. Even though they may trade up to a larger house as their family grows (and perhaps take on additional debt), their usual plan is to end up mortgage-free at retirement. Entering retirement, most couples and a high percentage of singles own their homes. In 2013, about 60 percent of households age 65–74 were mortgage free.[11] For those who still had a mortgage, the outstanding amount had been substantially reduced. For most households, home equity is the only significant nonpension saving. But retirees generally hold on to their home, and many leave it as a bequest.[12]

Since we do not save enough on our own and are not currently tapping home equity, the only place we can generate income for retirement is through two organized savings programs: Social Security and 401(k)s. What can we expect from these sources?

EXPECT LESS FROM SOCIAL SECURITY

During the 1980s and 1990s, Social Security benefits took households a long way toward meeting the 75 percent income replacement goal. At that time, the replacement rate from Social Security for the typical earner at 65 was about 40 percent. If that earner had a nonemployed wife, the Social Security benefit rose to 60 percent. Add any employer-sponsored pension income to that base and the total replacement rate would match or exceed the 75 percent target.

But future Social Security benefits will be very different from past benefits because of two major developments. First, under current law, the replacement rate for the individual worker at any given retirement age will be lower and, as we explain below, as more women work, *household* replacement rates will also decline. Second, the system's long-run financing problem is reaching the point at which Congress will be forced to make changes. Combine the already legislated reductions with potential additional cuts— to close the financing gap—and Social Security benefits will replace a much smaller share of preretirement incomes than they did in the past.

Declining Replacement Rates

Replacement rates will decline for three reasons: (1) the phasing in of already legislated benefit cuts; (2) increases in Medicare premiums; and (3) taxation of Social Security benefits.

Legislated Benefit Cuts

As noted earlier, the retirement age for receiving maximum monthly Social Security benefits is now 70. But scheduled increases in the program's so-called Full Retirement Age from 65 to 67 are cutting benefits across the board. For those who continue to retire at 65, this cut takes the form of lower monthly benefits; for those who choose to work longer, it takes the form of fewer years of benefits. For the typical earner who retires at 65, the replacement rate will drop from about 40 percent today to 36 percent once the transition is complete. (Comparable declines will also occur for low and high earners.)

Medicare

The second factor that will reduce future replacement rates is the rising cost of Medicare, since Medicare premiums are automatically deducted from Social Security benefits. Part B premiums are scheduled to increase from 5.4 percent of the average Social

Security benefit for someone retiring in 1990 to 10.4 percent for someone retiring in 2030.[13] Moreover, since premiums are scheduled to rise rapidly after retirement, they will account for an even larger share of Social Security benefits as recipients age, potentially consuming most of the cost-of-living adjustments provided along the way.[14]

Taxation

The third factor that will reduce Social Security benefits is the extent to which they are taxed under the personal income tax. Individuals with more than $25,000 and married couples with more than $32,000 of "combined income" pay taxes on up to 85 percent of their Social Security benefits.[15] In 1985, only about 10 percent of Social Security beneficiaries had to pay taxes on their benefits, but the percentage of people subject to tax has been increasing over time.[16] Today, about 37 percent of households pay taxes on their benefits, and by 2030 that will increase to more than 50 percent.[17]

Combined Impact for Individuals

For the average worker retiring at 65, the combined impact on the replacement rate of raising the Full Retirement Age from 65 to 67, the rising Medicare premiums, and the taxation of a portion of Social Security benefits will reduce the replacement rate by nearly a quarter—from a net 40 percent in 1985 to 31 percent by 2030 (see figure 3.3).[18] (If the worker retires at 62 as soon as benefits become available, the replacement rate would be even lower.)

Impact of Married Women Working

Most people retire as married couples, sharing and replacing a common household income. Thus, to get a real sense of the role of Social Security in the nation's retirement income system, we need

Figure 3.3. Social Security Is Shrinking

Social Security Replacement Rates for Average Earner Retiring at Age 65, 1985, 2000, 2015, and 2030

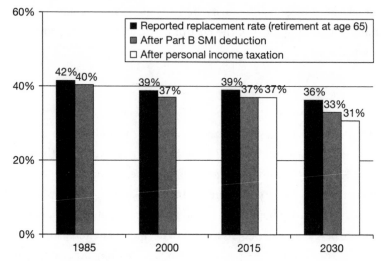

Sources: Centers for Medicare and Medicaid Services (2013); US Social Security Administration (2013b).

to consider the replacement rate of couples—as opposed to individual earners—and how that rate is changing. Years ago, when most women did not work, the wife who claimed at 65 was entitled to a benefit equal to 50 percent of her husband's. So, for example, for a beneficiary with a replacement rate of 40 percent, the replacement rate for a couple was 60 percent.

As women have gone to work, the couple's replacement rate has declined.[19] If the wife's earnings are modest relative to her husband's, the decline is small. As the wife's earnings rise relative to the husband's, the couple's replacement rate declines further. When the husband and wife have the same earnings, the couple's replacement rate drops to 40 percent, the same level as a single individual. Between 1980 and 2010, a rising ratio of wife's to husband's earnings reduced the replacement rate for the average couple by three percentage points.

In short, forces already in place will substantially reduce Social Security's contribution to the 75 percent replacement rate target. And if benefits are cut to eliminate the program's 75-year deficit, the reduction could be even greater.

The 75-Year Shortfall

By law, Social Security cannot spend money it does not have. Therefore, if nothing is done before the trust fund reserves are exhausted in 2033, Social Security benefits would be cut by about 25 percent to match benefits going out with taxes coming in. The replacement rate for the typical worker aged 65 would drop from 36 percent to 27 percent—a level not seen since the 1950s. Such an outcome would create a major problem.

Let's step back and take a closer look at Social Security' finances. Each year, the Social Security actuaries project the system's financial outlook over the next 75 years. They make projections under three sets of assumptions—high cost, low cost, and intermediate. The intermediate assumptions show the cost of the program rising rapidly to about 17 percent of taxable payrolls in 2035, where it remains for several decades until drifting up slightly to 18 percent (see figure 3.4). This increase is driven by demographics. As baby boomers retire and the ratio of retirees to workers rises from 35 per hundred workers to nearly 50 per hundred workers, pay-as-you-go costs increase commensurately. This increase is not news; actuaries have known about the baby boom for a long time.

Note that the baby boom is not "a pig in a python"—a large cohort just passing through and once the last member dies, life returns to normal. Costs will stay high due to the long-term

Figure 3.4. Social Security Faces a Shortfall

Projected Social Security Income and Cost Rates, as a Percentage of Taxable Payroll, 1990–2088

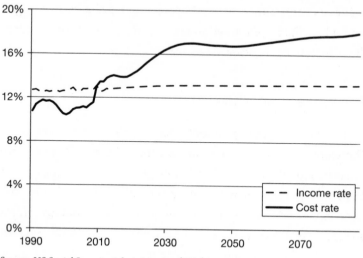

Source: US Social Security Administration (2014).

increases in life expectancy and the stabilization of the birth rate. The baby boom is noteworthy only because it explains the unprecedented speed at which costs increase over the next two decades.

While costs rise over the next two decades and stay high, income to the Social Security program remains a constant percentage of payroll. Rising costs and constant revenues produce the 75-year shortfall.[20] Over the next 75 years, the gap between projected benefits and revenues (and trust fund assets) will amount to a projected 2.88 percent of covered earnings.[21] So, if payroll taxes were raised immediately by 2.88 percentage points—1.44 percentage points each for both the employee and the employer—we could pay the current package of benefits for everyone who reaches retirement age through 2088. Alternatively, eliminating the entire 75-year deficit solely by reducing benefits would require a 17.4 percent cut right now—or a 20.8 percent cut if the reductions were limited only to new beneficiaries.

If nothing is done until the trust funds are depleted in 2033, the payroll tax would have to be increased by 4.2 percentage points at that point, with the increase rising to 5.3 percentage points by 2088. Or, alternatively, benefits could be cut to match scheduled taxes; this option would require a 23 percent cut in 2033, rising to 28 percent in 2088.

The bottom line on Social Security is clear: under current law, replacement rates will be much lower than those enjoyed by our parents, *and* they could be reduced even further if policymakers do not increase program revenues.

401(K)S COME UP SHORT

With declining replacement rates from Social Security, employer-sponsored retirement plans become much more important. Unfortunately, only about half of private sector workers—at any particular time—are participating in any form of employer-sponsored plan, and this share has remained relatively constant over the last 30 years (see box 3.2). The lack of universal coverage means that many American workers move in and out of plan participation and a significant percentage will end up with nothing but Social Security.

For those lucky enough to work for an employer providing a retirement plan, the nature of employer-sponsored plans has changed dramatically over the last 30 years. As noted in chapter 2, in the early 1980s most covered workers had a defined benefit plan that pays a lifetime benefit based on salary and length of service; today most workers have a 401(k) as their primary or their only

Box 3.2 how big is the pension participation gap?

The size of the pension participation gap has become a controversial question recently. Some commentators downplay the problem, citing a Labor Department survey of employers—the National Compensation Survey (NCS)—showing that about 80 percent of workers have access to a plan. However, household surveys consistently show that participation rates are in the 40–55 percent range. What accounts for the differences? It turns out that the devil is in the definition—of who, and what, is being measured.

To reconcile the numbers, it helps to compare the NCS employer survey to a Labor Department survey of households—the Current Population Survey (CPS) (see table 3.2). The NCS shows that, in 2012, 78 percent of employers, public and private, *offer* pensions to full-time workers ages 25–64. Excluding public sector workers (who essentially have universal coverage) lowers the figure slightly to 74 percent. Add in part-time workers (who, after all, will still need to save for retirement) and the number drops to 64 percent. Finally, using the percentage of workers who actually *participate* in a plan, rather than those who are *offered* one, reduces the total to 48 percent. This figure compares to 43 percent for the same definition in the CPS, still a difference but only a modest one. In the end, it seems reasonable to conclude that about half of private sector workers participate in a retirement plan.

Table 3.2 Only One-Half of Private Sector Workers Participate in Pensions

Percentage of Workers (25–64) With Pensions in the CPS and NCS, 2012

Category	CPS	NCS
Employer offers, public and private, full-time	63%	78%
Employer offers, private, full-time	59%	74%
Employer offers, private, full-time and part-time	52%	64%
Employee participates, private, full-time and part-time	43%	48%

Source: Munnell and Bleckman (2014).

plan. This shift means the employee rather than the employer makes all the decisions *and* bears all the risks.[22] In theory, workers should be able to accumulate substantial balances in 401(k)s, but in practice—as we now know—many workers do not. Some fail to participate; and most who do participate contribute less than they should, do not diversify their investments, and cash out balances when changing jobs. The dramatic result: most workers will retire with far too little. (Box 3.3 describes one reason—low financial literacy—why individuals make mistakes with 401(k)s.)

The Pension Protection Act of 2006

To help make 401(k) plans easier and more automatic, Congress enacted the Pension Protection Act of 2006 (PPA). Many of the PPA's provisions built on a series of behavioral studies that demonstrated that inertia plays a major role in how workers decide to

Box 3.3 many americans lack basic financial literacy

Extensive evidence shows that Americans lack basic levels of financial literacy. As just one example, in a recent study, researchers asked a nationally representative sample of Americans three questions.[23]

1. *Suppose you had $100 in a savings account and the interest was 2 percent per year. After five years, how much do you think you would have in the account if you left your money to grow? More than $102, exactly $102, or less than $102?*
2. *Imagine that the interest rate on your savings account was 1 percent per year and inflation was 2 percent per year. After one year, how much would you be able to buy with the money in the account? More than today, exactly the same, or less than today?*
3. *Buying a single company's stock usually provides a safer return than a stock mutual fund. True or false?*

The first two questions are aimed at fundamental economic concepts related to saving; the third evaluates the respondent's understanding of risk diversification, a concept crucial for investing.

The answers seem so simple—more than, less than, and false. Yet among those ages 51–65, the percentage answering the three questions correctly was only 69 percent, 78 percent, and 60 percent, respectively. Only 41 percent got all three right. (The results were worse for both those younger and older!)

participate and invest in 401(k)s.[24] So the PPA provisions encouraged automatic enrollment, fostered automatic increases in deferral rates, and improved default investment options.[25]

Automatic Enrollment

The major innovation to encourage participation is automatic enrollment.[26] This one simple change—employees must "opt out" rather than "opt in"—can increase participation by about 40 percentage points, boosting participation rates to about 85–90 percent of employees.[27] And after three or four years, the vast majority of those automatically enrolled continue participating.[28] The PPA established a "safe harbor" so that employers adopting automatic enrollment can meet 401(k) antidiscrimination rules (which are designed to ensure that plans do not unduly favor high-wage employees) if they follow certain requirements.[29] With the PPA in place, the share of plans with auto-enrollment increased substantially at first, but has now stabilized at less than half (see figure 3.5). And given that employers typically auto-enroll only new employees, the effect on overall plan participation is much less than it should be.

Increases in Default Contribution Rates

One problem with automatic enrollment is that the same inertia that makes the approach effective for participation can lock people into low levels of contributions.[30] The typical "default" contribution rate is only 3 percent,[31] and, left on their own, people tend to stay at this low level of contribution. To combat this problem, the PPA's safe harbor provisions require employers to increase a participant's contribution rate by at least one percentage point annually up to 6 percent of compensation. Employers also have the option of increasing the default rate further, up to 10 percent.[32]

Figure 3.5. Auto-401(k)s Are No Longer Rare, But Still Not Prevalent

Percentage of 401(k) Plans with Automatic Enrollment and Automatic Escalation, 2012

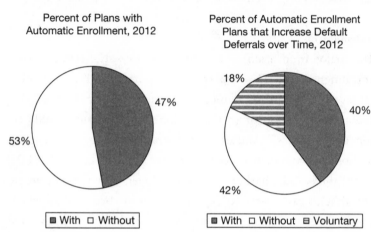

Source: Plan Sponsor Council of America (2013).

Unfortunately, only 40 percent of plans with automatic enrollment have automatic escalation in the default contribution, so many who are enrolled at low contribution rates remain at those low rates.[33]

Investment Options

The third problem that the PPA addressed was poor investment choices.[34] First, given inertia, many participants who were defaulted into stable value funds or money market funds remained in these investments. These funds are fine for savings and safety, but they are *not* long-term investments; they produce low returns, particularly net of inflation. Second, plan participants rarely rebalance their portfolios to maintain a chosen level of risk when values change significantly or to reflect changes in their own preferred risk level as they get older. To address these problems, the PPA defined a list of "qualified default investment alternatives" that include target date funds, balanced funds, and managed accounts. Plans that place a participant's defaulted contributions in any of these investments avoid any fiduciary liability. (The liability shifts to the participant.) This legislation has had a major impact. Target date funds, where the share of assets allocated to stocks declines as people approach retirement, have replaced stable value and money market funds as the major "default" option. In 2012, 84 percent of 401(k) plans offered target date funds *and* more than half of all participants used these funds.[35]

401(k) Plans Still Come Up Short

Many thought that the Pension Protection Act would solve the problems associated with saving and investing in 401(k) plans. But data from the Federal Reserve's 2013 Survey of Consumer Finances—a triennial survey of a nationally representative sample of US households with detailed information on their assets—say otherwise.[36]

- Despite the increase in the share of plans with auto-enrollment since the PPA, about 20 percent of those eligible *still* do not participate in their employer's 401(k) plan. While many are younger workers, who face competing demands on their income, delaying participation in a 401(k) plan seriously reduces the likelihood that they will ever be adequately prepared for retirement.[37]
- Only about 10 percent of participants contribute as much as they are allowed to their 401(k) plans.[38] (In 2013, most employees were entitled to contribute $17,500

on a tax-deductible basis to their 401(k) plan. Workers approaching retirement could contribute another $5,500 under "catch-up" provisions introduced in 2002.) Not surprisingly, high earners are more likely to contribute the maximum than low earners.[39]

- About a third of participants fail to diversify their investments. Some overinvest in company stock, which—while a nice sign of loyalty—is a serious mistake since workers are already heavily committed—or "invested" in—the company for their earnings.[40]

- Except for those with target date funds, participants do not rebalance their portfolios as they age or in response to market returns.

- About 1.5 percent of assets each year leaks out of 401(k) plans when participants cash out as they change jobs, take hardship withdrawals, withdraw funds after age 59½, or default on loans. Such withdrawals can represent a rational financial decision for households facing hardships, but they still reduce retirement saving.[41]

As a result, in 2013, the median household approaching retirement with a 401(k) had a total of only $111,000 in 401(k) and IRA balances (see table 3.3).[42] IRA balances are included because the bulk of the money in IRAs has been rolled over from 401(k) accounts. The 2013 balances were *below* those in 2007 and 2010. If a retired couple consumes 4 percent of $111,000 each year, they receive less than $400 per month, adjusted for inflation—usually their only source of additional income other than Social Security. (As discussed earlier, the typical household holds almost *no* financial assets outside of its 401(k) plan or IRA.)

Table 3.3 401(k)/IRA Savings Are Low
401(k)/IRA Balances for Median Working Household with a 401(k), Age 55–64, by Income Quintile, 2013

Income range (quintiles)	Median 401(k)/IRA balance	Percentage with 401(k)
Less than $39,000	$13,000	22%
$39,000–$60,999	$53,000	48%
$61,000–$90,999	$100,000	60%
$91,000–$137,999	$132,000	65%
$138,000 or more	$452,000	68%
Total	**$111,000**	**52%**

Source: Authors' calculations from US Board of Governors of the Federal Reserve System, Survey of Consumer Finances (2013).

More Problems Down the Road

So far, policymakers have focused on the accumulation phase of 401(k) plans. But the first cohort of retirees dependent on 401(k) payouts is about to retire, and they face an enormous challenge: deciding how fast to draw down their retirement assets. Moreover, the discussion has focused almost exclusively on 401(k)s, while the bulk of 401(k) money has been rolled over into IRAs.

Payouts

Since 401(k) plans shift most of the responsibility for retirement planning from employers to employees, employees have to decide whether or not to participate in the plan, how much to contribute, how to invest the money, and whether to roll over lump-sum distributions into another retirement plan when changing jobs. Hard as they are, all these decisions are relatively easy compared to deciding how much to withdraw from 401(k) balances each year in retirement. Retirees face the risk of either spending too quickly and outliving their resources or spending too conservatively and depriving themselves of necessities or modest pleasures. (These risks could be eliminated through the purchase of annuities, but the annuity market for individuals in the United States is tiny and costly for the average person, as discussed in chapter 4.) So, once again, individuals are on their own. While it's too early to tell what they will do, the prospects are not encouraging.

Individual Retirement Accounts

IRAs now hold more assets than 401(k)s (see figure 3.6), due in large part to the rollover of past 401(k) balances into IRAs. Two concerns arise with this migration. First, people are moving from a protected world to an unprotected one. With 401(k) plans, employers must act as a fiduciary, putting the welfare of the participant first. No such fiduciary standards currently apply to IRAs. Similarly, the Department of Labor now requires employers with 401(k)s to disclose to participating employees the fees associated with various investment options in an understandable format. No such disclosure is required of IRAs.

The second issue pertains to policy reforms. For example, one option is to establish an automatically annuitized default in 401(k) plans. (As in all defaults, those who want a lump sum could opt out.) This kind of change, however, would have little impact in a world where more than half the assets are in IRAs, and more could

Figure 3.6. IRAs Hold More Assets Than 401(k)s

Private Retirement Assets, Trillions of Dollars, 2013 Q3

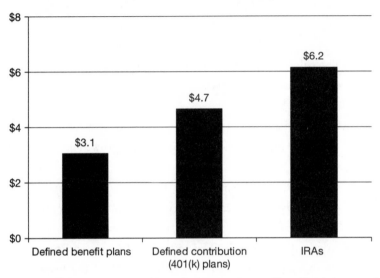

Source: US Board of Governors of the Federal Reserve System, *Flow of Funds Accounts of the United States* (2013b).

move to these accounts if participants did not like annuitization. So reform policy changes that affect only 401(k)s are too limited.

HIGHER AND LOWER INCOME HOUSEHOLDS

The focus so far has been on the average worker, as the simplest way of describing major trends, but it is also important to look at the pressures on households with lower and higher incomes. These groups will have quite different experiences since the Social Security benefit structure is progressive in that it replaces a greater share of earnings for the lower paid than for the higher paid (see box 3.4).

Box 3.4 social security's progressive benefit formula

The calculation of the Social Security benefit for a retired worker is a three-step process.

1. Restate the worker's previous earnings in terms of today's wages by indexing past earnings to wage growth up to age 60.
2. Average indexed earnings for the highest 35 years and divide by 12 to calculate Average Indexed Monthly Earnings (AIME).
3. Apply the benefit formula to the AIME to calculate the Primary Insurance Amount (PIA). In 2014, the benefit formula was:
   90 percent of the worker's first $816 of AIME, plus
   32 percent of AIME over $816 through $4,917, plus
   15 percent of any AIME in excess of $4,917.

This PIA is recalculated as long as the individual remains employed; it is indexed to prices from age 62.

The monthly benefit that a retired worker actually receives depends on when the worker claims. Highest benefits are paid at age 70, and benefits claimed earlier are reduced.

Low Earner ($21,100 in 2014)

Low-income workers rely more heavily on Social Security than other income groups for two reasons: they are less likely to be covered by an employer plan, and, as shown in box 3.4, the Social Security benefit formula provides them with higher benefits relative to earnings than the average earner. While 40 percent is the approximate benchmark replacement rate for the average worker retiring at 65, the approximate benchmark for low earners is 60 percent.

With the increase in the so-called Full Retirement Age, the replacement rate for low earners is scheduled to decline to 49 percent—a level not seen since the 1960s. Moreover, low earners tend to retire early, at 62, when Social Security benefits first become available. These benefits claimed early are actuarially reduced to keep lifetime benefits roughly equal for early and late claimers. As a result, the replacement rate for low earners who claim benefits at 62 will be only 39 percent.

Maximum Earner ($117,000 in 2014 and Higher)

Those earning at Social Security's taxable maximum—the maximum earnings considered for payroll taxes and benefits—have always received relatively low replacement rates, reflecting the progressive benefit formula. As the Full Retirement Age increases, the replacement rate for maximum earners will decline from 29 percent to 24 percent.

The higher-paid workers will have to rely mainly on saving through 401(k)s to reach the 75 percent target. In 2013, households approaching retirement in the top fifth of the income distribution had $452,000 in their 401(k)/IRA accounts (see table 3.3). That may sound like a lot of money, but withdrawing 4 percent annually would produce a monthly income of only $1,500 per month, adjusted for inflation—a replacement rate of only 8 percent for a person earning twice the maximum while working.

A COMPREHENSIVE MEASURE OF THE PROBLEM

Retirement needs are growing because of increasing life expectancy, low retirement ages, and soaring healthcare costs. At the same time, retirement incomes are going down because Social Security replacement rates are declining, investment returns are lower, and employer-sponsored plans are increasingly 401(k)s that only have modest balances. And few people are compensating for these reductions by saving more on their own. Unless major changes are made soon, millions of American workers will surely face a painful retirement income crunch.

A simple way to confirm that retirement prospects have worsened comes from a chart that shows the ratio of wealth to income at each age for each of the past 11 Surveys of Consumer Finances (see figure 3.7). Wealth includes all financial assets, including 401(k) accumulations, and housing *less* any outstanding debt. Income includes earnings and returns on financial assets.[43] The chart shows that the ratios for each age, from each survey, lie virtually on top of one another. At first, this regularity may seem comforting, suggesting that the cohorts that follow are as well prepared for retirement as their parents. But that conclusion is *wrong*.

Figure 3.7. We Need More Saving than Our Parents, But We're Not Doing It

Ratio of Wealth to Income by Age from the Survey of Consumer Finances, 1983–2013

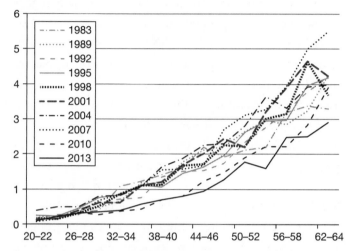

Source: Authors' calculations based on US Board of Governors of the Federal Reserve System, Survey of Consumer Finances (1983–2013).

While today's households have been accumulating wealth at much the same pace as their parents, the world has changed in five important ways discussed in this chapter:

1. Life expectancy has increased, so accumulated assets must support a longer period of retirement.
2. Social Security replacement rates have declined.
3. Defined benefit pension plans have been replaced by 401(k)s. (Note that accruals of future benefits under defined benefit plans are not included in reported wealth, while the buildup of assets in 401(k) plans is included.)
4. Healthcare costs have risen substantially and show signs of further increase.

5. Interest rates have fallen significantly from past record levels, so a given amount of wealth will now produce less retirement income.

These changes would be expected to lead to substantially higher wealth-to-income ratios if people were aiming to preserve their standard of living in retirement. Instead, the pattern of wealth accumulation has remained virtually unchanged, so people are increasingly *less* prepared for retirement.

To quantify the magnitude of the retirement income crunch, the Center for Retirement Research developed the National Retirement Risk Index.[44] The Index measures the percentage of working-age households who will not have saved enough money at retirement to maintain their preretirement standard of living. Figure 3.8 shows that the Index equaled 53 percent in 2010. That means 53 percent of working American households, roughly 35 million households, will not have enough retirement income to maintain their preretirement standard of living if they retire at age 65—which is later than the current average retirement age—and annuitize all their financial assets, including a reverse mortgage on their homes. In addition, a household must fall at least 10 percent short of its target to be considered unprepared for retirement.

Not surprisingly, 2010 showed a significant increase in the Index compared to 2007, due to the collapse of the housing market, stock prices, and real interest rates. But even taking into account the recovery in housing and stock prices that has occurred since 2010 would reduce the Index only modestly. More importantly, the long-term trend in retirement risk has been upward as a result of longer retirement spans, benefit cuts from increases in Social Security's Full Retirement Age, the shift to 401(k) plans, and the decline in interest rates. While this

Figure 3.8. Falling Short in Retirement Is Increasingly Likely
The National Retirement Risk Index, 1983–2013

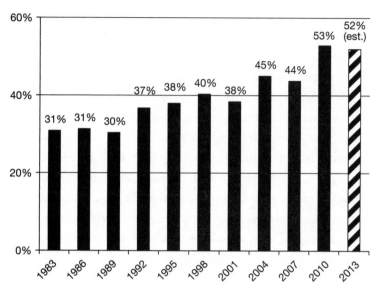

Source: Munnell, Rutledge, and Webb (2014 forthcoming).

Box 3.5 some believe retirement shortfalls are not a serious problem

While the evidence presented above suggests retirement shortfalls are a major problem, the question is not fully settled yet among academic researchers. For example, studies by well-respected scholars conclude that most Americans are saving optimally to meet their consumption needs in retirement, with less than 10 percent of households falling short.[45] The question is why this optimal savings approach yields such comforting results. The answer hinges on two key assumptions: (1) how

---

children affect replacement rate targets; and (2) how households consume their accumulated wealth in retirement.[46]

Children

What happens to household consumption once the children leave home? One hypothesis is that the adults keep household consumption steady by spending more on themselves, particularly on discretionary items such as travel, entertainment, and food. Under the optimal savings approach, though, the adults do not increase their spending; instead, they save the extra money that used to be devoted to their children. As a result, they have a lower replacement rate target and need to save less for retirement than households where consumption remains steady.

Retirement Drawdown

The second key assumption is how households consume their accumulated wealth in retirement. The NRRI has retirees buying an annuity so that they spend a steady inflation-adjusted amount. In contrast, the optimization model assumes that households draw down their wealth on their own. In this framework, households optimally choose higher consumption in their sixties, and significantly lower consumption by age 85. Households accept declining consumption in retirement because they are unwilling to save during their working years for consumption at ages when they are less likely to be alive. With a declining consumption path, the typical household will need to accumulate much less wealth to meet any target replacement rate at retirement.

The question then becomes which set of assumptions is most plausible. Spending does decline as people age, but it is unclear the extent to which the pattern reflects declining income; people cannot spend what they do not have. On the side of steady consumption, financial planning tools invariably assume that households require a level amount. The one study looking at how households react when the kids leave home finds that household consumption does not decline and per capita consumption increases. [47] But the sample size is small, so the issue is unresolved. The key point is that specific assumptions, with precise behavioral implications, are required to conclude that households are saving optimally.

evidence paints a clear picture of a major challenge, some academic researchers disagree (see box 3.5).

CONCLUSION

This chapter started by asking: "How big is the problem?" The answer is clear: the problem is substantial and getting worse. Unless we make changes, we are going to have an average of 20 years in retirement and face significant out-of-pocket health-care costs. Most of us do not save on our own, and we do not view our homes as potential sources of retirement income. So the story comes down to Social Security and 401(k) plans.

Social Security has served as the backbone of the nation's retirement system but, under current law, Social Security will provide less—relative to previous earnings—because of already scheduled benefit cuts, large deductions for Medicare premiums, and taxes on the gross benefit. In addition, few couples will receive the full spousal benefit, so benefits on a household basis will be reduced even further. In terms of support from Social Security, then, we will be back to the 1950s and 1960s.

In the private sector, with the demise of defined benefit plans, we have to rely on 401(k)s. But most 401(k) plans leave all the major decisions up to us as individuals; and we make mistakes at each and every step in the process. The result: too many of us save far too little for retirement. The typical household approaching retirement had only $111,000 in 401(k)/IRA holdings in 2013. This modest amount is a major problem. Assuming that a household withdraws 4 percent annually, monthly income would amount to less than $400, adjusted for inflation—about $4,500 a year. Many participants are likely to be surprised and badly disappointed—stuck with too little when it's too late to change.

We need to acknowledge the situation *now* and take action *now* to solve our retirement income problem—or we will once again have a substantial number of older Americans living in poverty. The next chapter explores what we can do as individuals to enhance our financial security after we stop working. The chapter after that explores what we can do as a nation to advance this goal.

[4]

WHAT CAN WE DO *AS INDIVIDUALS*?

As individuals, we need to recognize two core realities: (1) accumulating enough money to maintain our standard of living in retirement has become an enormous challenge; and (2) far more than our parents, *we are on our own*. Given this situation, our options are simple to define but can be hard to put into practice. We know we should work longer but have no idea how much longer. We know we need to save more to supplement a contracting Social Security system, but we don't know how much to save and we find both saving and investing difficult. The alternative to working longer and/or saving more is having to accept a much lower standard of living in retirement. Fortunately, we do have levers we can pull. This chapter lays out specific steps that we, *as individuals*, can take to produce better outcomes at retirement.

WORK LONGER

At first blush, it may seem strange to say: "We need to reduce our retirement years in order to ensure our years in retirement." But it's not nearly as bad as it sounds. The "working longer" prescription is *not* about having no retirement at all; it's about beginning retirement later. And because life expectancy has increased dramatically over the past several decades, working longer does not mean having fewer years in retirement than people in the golden age of retirement security.[1]

Financial Advantages of Working Longer

A few additional years in the labor force can make a big difference. Extending our work life produces current income; it leads to a large increase in monthly Social Security benefits; it allows us to contribute more to our 401(k) and for our balances to earn investment income; and it shortens the length of retirement, reducing the savings we'll need to maintain our standard of living (see figure 4.1). By and large, those who continue to work

Figure 4.1. Working Longer Helps Retirement Security in Three Ways
Impact of Working Longer on Social Security, 401(k)s, and the Retirement Span

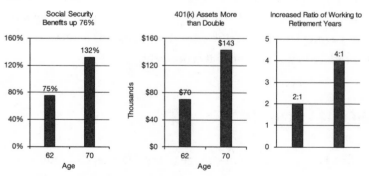

Source: Authors' calculations, using Vanguard (2013) 401(k) holdings by age for the middle panel.

beyond their mid-sixties should have a reasonably comfortable retirement.

Spending a few more years in the labor force greatly increases monthly Social Security benefits. Under the program's current structure, participants can start collecting benefits at any age between 62 and 70.[2] But, to maintain fairness, benefits claimed before 70 are actuarially reduced so *lifetime* benefits are made roughly equal for both early and late claimers. These adjustments are very significant. *Monthly* benefits for those who start claiming Social Security benefits at 70 are a *full 76 percent higher* than for those who start taking benefits at age 62 (see table 4.1). (If working longer also raises the average level of our 35 years of earnings used in the Social Security benefit calculation—which it probably will—the increase could be even greater.)

In addition to providing a higher monthly benefit, claiming Social Security later is particularly attractive for married couples. The reason: the survivor's benefit, unlike the spouse's benefit, depends on when the higher earner—historically, the husband—starts receiving benefits.[3] Widows (and widowers) get the higher of their own or their spouse's monthly benefit. So, the later the

Table 4.1 Claiming Later Boosts Benefits—a Lot!
Illustrative Monthly Social Security Benefit by Claiming Age

Claiming age	Monthly benefit	Gain
70	$1,760	76%
67	$1,440	44%
65	$1,245	25%
62	$1,000	

Source: Authors' calculations from US Social Security Administration (2013b).

husband claims Social Security, the higher his benefit *and* the higher the benefit his wife will receive after he dies. Thus, working longer and claiming benefits later greatly improves the benefits for both the worker *and* the spouse.

How to Work Longer

Working longer is not simple; it requires thought and planning. First, we need to take stock of our financial situation and determine how long to work. Most people who do this task will conclude that they want to keep working well beyond 65 to avoid risking a significant reduction in their living standard at retirement. Most will also conclude that remaining employed that long will be challenging.[4]

Second, we need to plan a way to extend our working careers. The best thing we can do is keep our skills up to date and be responsive to the needs of our employer. Human resource managers say that flexibility and the mastery of needed technical skills are the major concerns that employers have about their over-50 employees.[5] Remaining flexible and responsive is a question of attitude, of thinking "young." Keeping skills up to date requires the investment of time, effort, and perhaps even money for tuition. But it's worth it for an extra decade of productive activity.

Third, we need to make sure our employer knows about our target retirement age *and* our commitment to work so that it will make sense to invest in our skills and development to keep us productive into our late sixties. So, when we're in our fifties, we should let our employers know that they can count on us for another 15 or more years. (Americans have not been very successful in planning their retirement age. Surveys consistently find that workers *plan* on retiring later than they actually do.[6] So we should try to make a plan and stick to it.)

Fourth, we should try to keep working full time with our current employer, because our market value is usually greatest with an employer who knows us and values our skills. Changing jobs—let alone changing industries, occupations, or geographic locations—can sharply reduce earnings.[7] Downshifting to a less intensive job might sound attractive, but, if something goes wrong, it can be hard to reverse course and return to higher intensity and higher wage employment later. Similarly, moving from full-time to part-time might seem appealing, but many employers find part-time employees more expensive and less efficient. In short, be cautious about opting for anything other than regular, full-time employment.

Finally, we need to stay healthy. Age brings aches, pains, and maladies that can impair productivity and ability to work. We need to be more responsible for our health and well-being than when we were younger and our body did a better job of caring for itself. Good health will not only improve our quality of life but also make it possible to work longer and thereby reduce the need for retirement assets.

SAVE MORE

The second option to improve our prospects for a financially secure retirement is to save more. Easy to say, but hard to do. This goal requires not only putting more aside each year and investing wisely but also allocating assets across retirement years in the most effective way and taking advantage of all sources of saving—including our home equity. The challenge is great since we are not hardwired to save, we face enormous college costs, and the

Table 4.2 Most US Households Have Modest Incomes, Even Late in Their Careers

Income of Working Households, Age 55–64, by Income Quintile, 2013

Income quintile	Income range
Lowest	Less than $39,000
Second	$39,000–$60,999
Third	$61,000–$90,999
Fourth	$91,000–$137,999
Highest	$138,000 or more

Source: US Board of Governors of the Federal Reserve System, Survey of Consumer Finances (2013).

amounts required for retirement are very large due to longer life spans and rising healthcare costs.

Before exploring each of these challenges, it is worth noting that most Americans don't earn that much to begin with, which makes the task of saving more difficult. Even just considering households that are late in their careers, two of every five have incomes below $61,000, and only one in five makes more than $138,000 (see table 4.2).

Saving Is Hard

The economist's theoretical model of saving assumes individuals can forecast their needs decades into the future *and* have the discipline to act on those forecasts. To properly forecast retirement needs and how much we need to save, we would have to predict our earnings over our lifetimes, how long we will be able to work, how much we will earn on our assets, and how long we will spend in retirement. These forecasts are tough to make, even for experts, and most of us have great difficulty thinking far ahead on these questions. In a 2014 survey, 36 percent of respondents had not saved *anything* for retirement, and 56 percent had not even tried to figure out how much they might need.[8] We should all recognize that we are not good at planning for retirement.

Behavioral economics—which brings together economics, finance, and psychology—helps explain why we do not prepare well for retirement.[9] Not surprisingly, one problem is myopia; we are absorbed in our daily routines or prefer not to think of our own old age, so we fail to see what lies in the future. Most people don't even try. Those who do think about the future may plan to save next year, but when next year comes around, they don't take the necessary actions to fulfill their own plans.[10] Then, when approaching retirement, they reluctantly acknowledge that when younger they consumed far too much and saved far too little.

Another very human problem is self-control.[11] Inertia and procrastination—"I never get around to it"—are major components of our discipline problem. Some reasons for inaction are obvious: saving for a secure retirement tomorrow involves sacrificing consumption today; saving too little has no immediate visible penalty; and the process of saving seems complicated. And as the complexity of a task increases, we put off making decisions.[12]

Because we lack discipline, we need devices that force us to put money aside. That's why some people purposely have employers over-withhold on personal income tax to get a large refund at tax time, even though it gives the government an interest-free loan in the meantime. But most of our forced savings comes through employer-based retirement plans that regularly take money out of our paychecks and through monthly payments to pay off the mortgage on our home. In fact, virtually all saving is now done through employer-sponsored plans and home mortgages.

Experience shows that making saving easy and automatic is the only way to make it happen. A recent commitment device, which builds on these principles, can help people to reach their goal. While increasing employees' annual contributions is widely recognized as a very good thing, many employees find it hard to save more *today*. So behavioral economists have proposed Save More Tomorrow or SMART plans.[13] They work because employees agree to have an increasing percentage of pay—*after* their *next pay increase*—contributed to their 401(k) plan, reducing the pain of saving more today while increasing their investment in their own retirement security. As individuals, we should all ask our employers to offer such a plan *and* we should use it.

Competition from College Costs

In addition to not being hardwired to prepare for the future, rising college costs are making it increasingly difficult to save for retirement. The percentage of young people going to college has increased dramatically; the price of college has risen relative to family income; and these expenses are being incurred closer to parents' retirement because women are having children later. These developments affect future retirees in two ways. First, students take on large amounts of student loans and then often spend their twenties and thirties paying off that debt. (Two-thirds of college graduates have student loan debt, and the average debt is $29,400.[14] In fact, student loan debt now exceeds credit card debt.) The need to pay off student loans could lead some young workers to delay joining or participating fully in their employer's 401(k)—or put off buying a house. The alternative is for parents to pay the college costs, reducing their ability to save for their own retirement. This response protects the young, but endangers the parents' security.

Retirement Is Expensive

The long bull market of the 1980s and 1990s—when stock market returns averaged an astounding 13 percent per year—lulled many into thinking that saving for retirement was easy and that the typical contribution to 401(k) plans—6 percent from the employee with a 3 percent match from the employer—would be adequate. Not anymore! So we need to define realistic saving rates to meet the 75 percent target replacement rate discussed in chapter 3. The required rate depends on four factors:

1. Earnings. The higher our earnings, the smaller the proportion provided by Social Security and the higher our own required saving rate.
2. Age when saving starts. The earlier we start saving, the lower the required rate of saving needed for any given retirement age.
3. Age at retirement. The later we retire, the lower our required saving rate.
4. Rate of return. The higher the rate of return on our investments, the lower our required saving rate.

To figure out how much we need to save first requires determining how much we will get from Social Security. Under current law, Social Security ultimately will replace about 41 percent of preretirement earnings at age 67 for the typical worker. Subtracting that replacement rate from the target 75 percent determines how much we must save on our own. As most saving is done through employer-sponsored plans—primarily 401(k)s—the required saving rate is the combined employer-employee contribution rate. The final issue is to determine how much income can be drawn from our retirement savings. The calculations assume the "4 percent rule," often used by financial planners, whereby people annually withdraw an inflation-adjusted 4 percent of their wealth at retirement with the expectation that they will not exhaust their savings.[15] Of course, the 4 percent rule is not the only possible strategy; a higher drawdown rate, which would expose households to a greater risk of running out of money, would produce lower required saving rates and balances.[16]

Table 4.3 shows the required saving rate for different starting dates and retirement dates. This should not be viewed as a financial planning tool, but rather as a transparent way of showing the impact on the savings rate required by a combination of a specific starting age, retirement age, rate of return, and earnings.[17] Take the example of someone who earns the average wage ($46,830 in 2014) and retires at 67 in 2054. Under current law, Social Security will replace 41 percent of this person's final inflation-adjusted earnings. So, he has to save enough on his own to replace 34 percent (75 percent minus 41 percent). With the 4 percent rule, the average worker needs to accumulate investments of almost $630,000. If he starts saving at 35 and earns a real return—after inflation—of 4.6 percent, he will need to save 14 percent of earnings each and every year to be able to retire at 67 with financial security.

Two messages stand out. First, start dates and retirement dates are both very important, because *time* is so important. Starting to

Table 4.3 To Ease the Saving Burden, Start Early and Retire Late
Saving Rate Required for a Medium Earner to Attain a 75 Percent
Replacement Rate

Retire at	Start saving at		
	25	35	45
62	17%	29%	56%
65	12%	19%	35%
67	9%	14%	25%
70	5%	8%	14%

Note: The calculations assume a real rate of return of 4.6 percent and withdrawals based on the 4 percent rule. The target replacement rate drops from 75 percent for the medium earner to 70 percent for the maximum earner and to 65 percent for those earning twice the maximum.

Source: Authors' calculations.

save at age 25, rather than age 45, cuts the required annual saving rate by about two-thirds. And delaying retirement from age 62 to age 70 reduces the required annual saving rate by more than two-thirds—from 17 percent to 5 percent (or 29 percent to 8 percent for those who start at 35, or 56 percent to 14 percent for those who start at 45.) Taken together, starting at 25 and working to 70—compared to starting at 45 and retiring at 62—reduces the required annual saving rate by a factor of 10!

The second fact that stands out is disturbing: for retirement before age 70, virtually all of the required saving rates, even for those who start early, are in excess—usually far in excess—of today's typical contribution rate of 9 percent (6 percent employee contribution and 3 percent employer match) going into 401(k) plans.

A couple of comments. First, the calculations shown assume an inflation-adjusted real rate of return of 4.6 percent—reflecting a portfolio of half stocks and half bonds. Raising the assumed real (after inflation) return to 6 percent would reduce the required saving rates, but these "reduced" rates would still be higher than current 401(k) contribution rates. Lower assumed returns, however, would require even higher savings rates than those shown above. Second, the table shows the outcomes for the *average* worker; low earners *or* those earning Social Security's taxable maximum ($117,000 in 2014) differ because, as discussed, Social Security replaces a larger percentage of earnings at the low end and a smaller percentage for maximum earners. Those earning the taxable maximum, who retire at 70, will need to save between 8 to 21 percent of earnings—depending on when they start.[18] Those who earn more than the maximum will have to save even more, because Social Security will account for a smaller portion of their retirement income.

The main message is clear: retirement is expensive—and longer retirements are more expensive. People are going to need substantial assets if they are going to maintain their standard of living for many years after they stop working. Table 4.4 shows the size of the required assets relative to income for people at different earnings levels. With a retirement age of 62, the typical worker earning about $47,000 in 2014 will need assets at retirement of about 11 times his earnings—$524,500—while the person earning $234,000 (twice the Social Security taxable maximum) will need more than 13 times earnings—$3.1 million to maintain his standard of living.[19] These required amounts drop significantly if workers postpone their retirement to 70—the median worker needs only 6 times earnings ($267,000) and the person earning twice

Table 4.4 Retirement Is Expensive!
Multiple of Current Income Needed to Reach 75 Percent Replacement Rate
by Retirement Age, by Earnings

Annual Earnings	Age			
	62	65	67	70
Medium ($46,830)	11.2	9.4	8.2	5.7
Maximum ($117,000)	12.3	11.2	10.4	8.6
2× Maximum ($234,000)	13.4	12.9	12.4	11.6

Note: The calculations assume a real rate of return of 4.6 percent, wage growth of 1.2 percent, and withdrawals based on the 4 percent rule. The target replacement rate drops from
75 percent for the medium earner to 70 percent for the maximum earner and to 65 percent
for those earning twice the maximum.

Source: Authors' calculations.

the maximum less than 12 times ($2.7 million). Most American
workers are not on the pathway to anywhere near these amounts,
and most of us do not know how lost we are.

MAKE YOUR 401(K) PLAN WORK FOR YOU

Most of us will do the bulk of our saving though our 401(k)
plan. And, as just discussed, the earlier we start contributing
and the longer we wait to start withdrawing the funds, the lower
the required contribution rate. Therefore, our most important
steps are to join our employer's 401(k) plan as soon as possible and to contribute at least enough each year to receive the

full matching contribution from our employer. The only reason to postpone joining a 401(k) is excessive credit card debt. At 18 percent interest rates—the rate charged on credit card balances that are delinquent—the amount of money owed *doubles* in just four years—and then redoubles in the next four years. So pay off the credit card debt as soon as possible, and then join the 401(k) plan.

Invest Wisely

Investing is not easy. As humans, we tend to make lots of mistakes. All too often we decide on investments by looking in the rearview mirror: we sell stocks *after* the market drops and buy stocks *after* the market has gone up. This all-too-human behavior cuts the average investor's long-term return by about one-third. Even more destructive of long-term returns, investors can get so badly frightened by a severe bear market that they sell out at or near the bottom, thereby converting a short-term market loss into a permanent loss. In late 2007 and 2008, 401(k) and IRA investors lost over $1 trillion in market value—and then the market recovered. Those who stayed the course saw their balances rebound. But others panicked, sold out at the bottom, and got hurt badly.

We also fail to rebalance our portfolios in response to major market changes or as we age. When major market changes tilt the account's assets away from the optimal mix, it is important to sell assets that have increased as a share of the portfolio and buy those that have not. Such rebalancing keeps the riskiness of the portfolio reasonably consistent with the level of market risk that an individual can tolerate. Moreover, our tolerance for market risk will usually decline as we age—particularly with retirement and the end of earned income—so we also need to rebalance our portfolios to match changes in our risk preferences.[20]

Many of us, particularly those who work for employers with small 401(k) plans, pay too much in fees. And fees that may look small can have a big impact; an additional one percentage point in fees over a 40-year period reduces our assets at retirement by about one-fifth. One major change over the past 60 years has been the rise, maturity, and inevitable decline in the benefits to investors from retaining *active* investment managers. While active managers often achieved superior investment performance back in the 1960s, 1970s, and 1980s, the securities markets have changed. Increasing evidence shows that—because investment management pays very well and has attracted so many hard-working and highly skilled individuals with equal access to great information and computer power—active professional managers now dominate the securities markets. As a result, the markets are increasingly "efficient" or correctly priced, so that only a minority of managers outperform the markets each year.[21] Since the successful managers change from year to year, investors are unable to identify the long-term winners in advance. Yet, actively managed funds charge fees that are *10 times* the cost of index funds. So, *after fees*, indexing outperforms most active managers.[22] Few investment experts would willingly switch their own personal investments from indexing to active management. Increasingly, index funds are seen as the most efficient way to invest for many classes of equities and bonds; they deliver full market returns at no more risk and at lower cost. Participants in 401(k)s who work for large companies generally face even lower fees because large employer plans are often effective fee negotiators.

Some will argue for more investor education, but years of experience with noble efforts confirm that most of us are just too busy to make time to learn all we would need to know to be success-ful investors.[23] This reality is not going to change. Fortunately, the need for investor skills has been much reduced. In many cases, index funds achieve *superior* results at low cost, and target date funds offer a sensible answer to the *strategic* question of how to change the balance of stocks and bonds as we age and eventually retire *or* how to rebalance as markets go up or down. So if we stick to index funds and target date arrangements, we will be able to worry less and do better on the investing front.[24]

Keep the Money in the Plan

It's not good enough to put money into a 401(k) plan and invest it sensibly; we need to keep it there. To encourage participants to keep their money in the plan, the federal government has imposed a 10 percent penalty, in addition to regular income taxes, on withdrawals before age 59½. For tax purposes, employers are required to withhold 20 percent of any distributions paid directly to recipients.[25]

For those willing to pay the tax, 401(k) plans unfortunately offer a number of ways for participants to take their money out early.[26] The easiest is when changing jobs. Many younger people, in relatively low tax brackets, cash out their 401(k) balances when they move from one job to another. This pattern may seem harm-less because the amounts are generally relatively small, but over time compound interest turns small amounts into large amounts. The *Rule of 72* can be used to estimate how long it will take an investment to double at different rates of return. For example, assume a $100 investment that yields 6 percent. According to the Rule of 72, that amount will double in 12 years (72 ÷ 6) and redou-ble in another 12 years and redouble *again* in another 12 years. So,

$100 invested at age 30 can be thought of as $800 by age 66 or $1,600 by age 78—when it may be very much needed. So while the immediate loss of dollars is modest, the impact on final accumulations and retirement security is significant.

In addition, most plans allow participants to take money out in the event of a hardship before age 59½ (generally with a tax penalty) or under any circumstances after age 59½ (without a tax penalty). "Hardships" are broadly defined, including purchasing a primary residence, education, medical expenses, or general financial pressures. Most of those taking hardship withdrawals are in their forties and have a combination of mortgages, high credit card debt, and college expenses. While the percentage of participants taking hardship withdrawals is usually less than 2 percent per year, withdrawals increased noticeably after the financial crisis.[27] Moreover, to the extent that a different 2 percent of people are withdrawing money each year, a larger cumulative number of participants are affected. Except in severe hardship, it is a mistake to use our 401(k) plan as an "emergency fund." Putting money in and then taking it out at a penalty tax rate is expensive. A much better approach is for individuals to maintain a separate short-term savings account as a buffer against unanticipated expenses.

An increasingly used option is taking the money out of a 401(k) while still working—after age 59½—when the 10-percent penalty no longer applies. Ironically, elimination of the penalty may signal to people that 59½ is an appropriate age at which to withdraw funds. Fortunately, recent evidence suggests that most people taking these withdrawals roll over their money into IRAs—perhaps consolidating their accounts in advance of retirement. Nevertheless, about 30 percent appears to leave the system, suggesting that these withdrawals should be a source of concern, given that most of us will need to keep our retirement funds in the plan and growing for as long as possible.

Finally, most 401(k) plans allow participants to borrow up to 50 percent of their balances (up to a maximum of $50,000). These loans must be paid back within 5 years, or 10 years if used to purchase a primary residence. The impact of the loan on retirement savings depends on whether the borrowed money is used for an investment, such as building a garage, or for consumption, such as a vacation. Most people use their loans for home improvements or bill consolidation, and so are simply reshuffling their balance sheets.[28] The main potential concern from 401(k) borrowing is that borrowers stop making their regular plan contributions while paying back the loan, or worse, lose their jobs and are unable to pay back the loan. In this case, the loan then becomes a withdrawal— subject to income tax and the 10 percent penalty.

The bottom line is that the only way for 401(k) plans to function effectively is for participants to put in meaningful contributions and leave the money in the plan until retirement.

Be Careful about IRA Rollovers

When changing jobs, many people, who rarely change their contribution rate or rebalance their portfolios in response to market fluctuations or as they age,[29] suddenly get active in a major way and decide to "roll over" their 401(k) balances into an IRA. This behavior suggests a strong motivating force is at work.[30] That force is the barrage of advertisements and sales pitches from financial services firms urging participants to move their funds out of their "old," "tired" 401(k) plan into a new IRA.[31] Rolling over 401(k) balances into an IRA is definitely better than cashing out—because it at least keeps the money tax-sheltered—but it is not as good as leaving the money in the employer-sponsored plan, where participants are protected by fiduciary requirements and where a spotlight has now been focused on high management fees.

Withdraw Assets Effectively

We need to think carefully about how to spend our hard-earned savings after we retire. Since the payout from a 401(k) plan is likely to be in the form of a lump sum, we need a realistic financial plan that will balance the risks of spending too quickly and outliving our savings or spending too cautiously and consuming too little. Deciding on a realistic retirement withdrawal program will be one of the most important "money" decisions most of us will ever make. Once again, we are all on our own, but we have some options. Annuities are one possibility; some easy rules of thumb are another; and adopting the Internal Revenue Service's Required Minimum Distributions is a third possible approach.

Annuities

Annuities are contracts offered by insurance companies that pay a stream of monthly payments in exchange for a premium. The annuity not only protects people from outliving their resources but also allows more annual income than most could provide on their own. This fact may seem surprising, but the insurance company pools the experience of a large group of people and pays benefits to those who live longer than expected out of the premiums paid by those who die early. That is, pooling creates a "mortality premium."[32]

Economic theory suggests that rational people who do not plan to leave a bequest would always choose to annuitize 100 percent of their wealth, because they face a choice between a traditional investment with a market return and an annuity with a market return plus a "mortality premium."[33] The only drawback is that annuity payments stop at death, but that shouldn't be a problem if people are not interested in leaving a bequest.

In fact, most people don't buy annuities.[34] Some of our resistance to annuities comes from financial realities. We do care about leaving bequests. We already have a lot of annuitized wealth in the form of Social Security benefits, pension benefits, and the imputed rent from living in our home rent-free; and we want to have funds to cover any large out-of-pocket healthcare expense. Some of our resistance comes from the nature of the annuity product. Annuities are expensive for the average person because they have been priced for the typical annuity purchaser—an individual who lives into his nineties—and, being complicated, they require substantial marketing costs, which create high fees. Add concerns about the viability of insurance companies in the wake of the 2008 financial crisis, and some resistance is understandable. But some of the resistance to annuities is irrational—we value piles of wealth more than assured flows of income; some of us are afraid that we will hand over our money to an insurance company and then die the next day; and many of us simply don't understand the advantages of the product.[35] Regardless of the reason, most people are not going plunk down their $100,000 for a traditional annuity, so it's worth considering two alternatives—an ALDA and an annuity from Social Security.

ALDAs

An ALDA is an Advanced Life Deferred Annuity, sometimes called longevity insurance.[36] It is designed to ensure that we will have a steady income if we live to our mid-eighties or longer. ALDAs accomplish this goal by providing guaranteed income for life *after* the policyholder reaches an advanced age—typically around 85. The size of the payoff depends on the age at which the individual purchases the ALDA. Several companies currently sell these products.

Here's how ALDAs work, using the traditional annuity as a starting point. If an individual purchased a $100,000 traditional annuity at 65, he would immediately receive a stream of income of about $7,000 annually for life. But the purchase would leave the individual with no cash on hand for an emergency. With an ALDA, the individual could purchase the $7,000 income stream with payments *beginning* at age 85. Since the $7,000 annual payouts would not start until 20 years out in the future, the cost of an ALDA is substantially less—roughly $12,000.[37] So, out of the $100,000, the buyer would retain $88,000 to spend between 65 and 85.[38]

Of course, any product has drawbacks—some perceived and some real. As with all insurance, the purchaser gets to collect only if the event occurs. Homeowners collect on fire insurance only if their house catches on fire. Older people collect on ALDAs only if they live past 85. Unlike fire insurance, however, the purchaser cannot change his mind after a year and get the money back; the premium paid is locked in. Both these features are integral to the nature of the product. A more substantive concern is that existing ALDAs do not adjust for inflation. That failure means that the $7,000 received at age 85 will have lost a lot of its purchasing power. The lack of inflation protection, however, could be easily rectified if consumers had any interest in the product. But it remains to be seen whether the ALDA can overcome people's general aversion to annuities.

Annuity from Social Security
Another possibility—especially for those with 401(k)/IRA balances of $100,000 or so—is to "buy" an annuity from Social

Security.[39] Here's how: Social Security benefits are, in essence, inflation-protected annuities: they rise in line with prices and continue as long as we live.[40] We can "buy" an additional amount of this annuity by claiming benefits later.

"Buying" an annuity from Social Security is generally more attractive than buying a commercial annuity for several reasons. First, the Social Security annuity is designed to be "actuarially fair."[41] Commercial annuities, by contrast, cannot be "actuarially fair," because insurance companies have marketing, management, and risk-bearing costs that must be added to the price in addition to a profit. Second, Social Security benefit adjustments are based on the life expectancy of the "average" individual, which makes them less expensive than commercial annuities that are priced for those with above-average life expectancy (a characteristic of annuity buyers). Third, buying an annuity from Social Security is *especially* attractive when interest rates are as low as they are today, because, unlike an insurance company, Social Security doesn't reduce the annuity payout it offers when interest rates fall. So if we have to stop working because of health or lack of employment opportunities, it may make sense to use a portion of our 401(k)/IRA assets to cover living expenses for a few years and delay claiming Social Security.

Rules of Thumb for Drawing Down Assets

For any assets that are not annuitized, most people have traditionally used one of three rules of thumb to decide how much to spend in retirement. Since they each have drawbacks, we suggest a fourth alternative, discussed more fully below.[42]

The three traditional rules of thumb include using only the income produced by the assets, calculating withdrawals based on life expectancy, and adopting the so-called 4 percent rule.

- *Use cash income only.* This strategy leaves the principal in the retirement account untouched and spends only dividends and interest received. This approach may work for wealthy individuals who want to leave a substantial bequest, but for most of us it unnecessarily restricts retirement consumption. Another drawback is the potential to distort portfolio diversification, by overinvesting in dividend-yielding stocks in an effort to produce higher income.

- *Base withdrawals on life expectancy.* This strategy is to spend all our financial assets over our remaining life span based on actuarial tables of average life expectancy. While the calculation, if properly done, is not simple, a more serious problem is that averages are only averages, so each of us would have a 50 percent chance of outliving our savings and being forced to rely solely on Social Security.

- *Adopt the 4 percent rule.* Under the "4 percent rule" advocated by many financial planners, retirees each year withdraw 4 percent of their *initial* balance.[43] The advantage is the low probability of running out of money. However, such a rule does not encourage retirees to periodically adjust consumption in response to long-term investment returns. For example, if over several years, returns are less than expected, consumption should be reduced to preserve assets; when returns are more than expected, consumption could be increased. A fixed 4 percent withdrawal is not consistent with such flexibility.

An alternative to the traditional rules of thumb is to base withdrawals on the Required Minimum Distributions (RMD), which the Internal Revenue Service (IRS) requires for 401(k) and IRA balances when we reach age 70½ and each year thereafter.[44] The IRS makes no claim that the RMD, which is designed to recoup deferred taxes, produces an optimal drawdown strategy. Yet this approach satisfies four important tests of a good strategy: (1) it is easy to follow; (2) it allows the percentage of remaining wealth consumed each year to increase with age; (3) it does not encourage people to chase dividends by overinvesting in high-dividend stocks; and (4) it forces consumption to respond to fluctuations in the market value of the financial assets. The RMD also performs well compared to the traditional rules of thumb.[45] The percentages to be withdrawn each year under the RMD, with estimates for the years before 70½, are shown in table 4.5.[46]

This discussion of how to draw down retirement assets has been relatively long, because it is a major challenge to figure out how much to take out each year over an uncertain lifetime. Everyone retiring with 401(k)/IRA assets as the only supplement

Table 4.5 RMD Rules Offer a Reasonable Drawdown Strategy
IRS's Required Minimum Distribution Rules

Age	Percentage of assets to be withdrawn
65	3.13%
70	3.65%
75	4.37%
80	5.35%
85	6.76%
90	8.77%
95	11.63%
100	15.87%

Sources: Internal Revenue Service (2012); Sun and Webb (2012).

to Social Security is going have to figure out some way to solve this problem. Some form of annuity and/or reliable rules of thumb will be essential to balance the goals of securing an adequate income, on the one hand, and not running out of money, on the other.

USE HOME EQUITY

For most families, their house is their major asset—and also their largest expense. Owning a home allows us to live rent-free in retirement, without worrying about a landlord who could raise our rent or ask us to move. Generally, older people also think of their house as a reserve in case they face major health-related expenses such as the need for long-term care (see box 4.1).

The house is rarely considered as a source of income in retirement. In the absence of a precipitating event such as the death of a spouse or entry of a family member into a nursing home, most households continue to own their own home well into their eighties. Even when a financial shock occurs, selling the home is rare.[47] Households that do sell their home are likely to purchase another house and increase, rather than reduce, home equity. But the fact that households do not currently tap home equity does not mean that we should ignore this potential source of income in the future.

Homeowners can access their equity either by downsizing to a less expensive house or by taking out a reverse mortgage. Downsizing boosts the household's income in two ways: it adds to savings, which can be used to generate income or to delay claiming Social Security benefits, and it cuts expenses—taxes, insurance, upkeep, and utilities are all likely to be less with a cheaper

Box 4.1 a word on long-term care

The prospective costs for long-term care are a big problem that we all need to consider. First, nursing home care is really expensive for those who end up needing it. Second, the prospect of such an expense is likely to prevent people from making the best use of their meager 401(k) assets, much less tapping their home equity.

It would be nice if Americans had access to good long-term care insurance *and* bought the product. But despite the fact that over one-quarter of men and over two-fifths of women will enter a nursing home at some point after 65 *and* that a semiprivate room currently costs about $80,000 a year, only about 10 percent of households purchase long-term care insurance. One reason is that low-income households can get free long-term care under Medicaid. Others think—incorrectly—that nursing home care is fully covered under Medicare. And the current products are not very attractive. Long-term care insurance is expensive, and the insurance company can increase the premiums when interest rates fall. Those who, in response to higher costs, stop paying the premium will lose all protection. (Many insurance companies don't like this market any more than individuals; several major sellers have sharply reduced or discontinued sales since 2010.)[48]

Perhaps one way forward would be to develop a new type of long-term care product. We strongly favor a catastrophic policy with the premiums paid up front. This product would pay benefits only *after* the individual had paid for, say, 12 months of nursing home care, or $80,000. This arrangement would change an unbounded black hole of an expense into a known quantity. Moreover, the premium for this benefit would be relatively modest and could be paid in a single lump sum at retirement so buyers need not worry about premium costs climbing as they age. The hope would be that once people understood the dimensions of their exposure to long-term care costs, they would feel more comfortable about spending their balances and tapping their home equity. Unfortunately, such a product does not currently exist in the United States.[49]

house. In short, by reducing consumption of housing, downsizing frees up money to use for a retiree's other consumption needs. Downsizing may be a good option for those whose house is suited to an earlier stage in life, with rooms that are no longer used, near schools and playgrounds that are no longer needed, and close to an office where they no longer work. In this case, downsizing may actually improve the quality of life in retirement by providing the right number of rooms and a more maneuverable layout in a neighborhood that offers amenities more suitable for older people than young couples with families. If downsizing makes sense, then we should probably do it as soon as we can to halt the drain on our savings and to begin building our new life.

Older people who want to spend their retirement in their current home can tap their home equity and increase their retirement income through a reverse mortgage. A reverse mortgage is a loan available to homeowners 62 and over that allows them to borrow money using their house as collateral. (The money can be taken in the form of monthly payments, a line of credit, or in cash up to 60 percent of the total amount in the first year.) This product enables us stay in our house for the rest of our life without making any payments other than property tax or homeowner's insurance. Since the money is a loan, it is tax-free and does not affect costs pegged to income—such as Medicare premiums—or how Social Security benefits are taxed. The amount owed, which equals the amount the homeowner receives plus interest, needs to be repaid only when the homeowners move, sell their house, die, or fail to pay property taxes or homeowners insurance premiums.

Reverse mortgages have been criticized as being too expensive with high upfront fees.[50] In response to cost and other factors, the government recently revamped the entire Home Equity Conversion Mortgage (HECM) program.[51] Under the new regulations, those who take out less than 60 percent of the loan in the first year pay only 0.5 percent in mortgage insurance premiums. The new regulations also reduce somewhat the maximum amount of home equity that borrowers can access.[52] Yet, a 72-year-old can still withdraw up to 57.5 percent, minus fees.

Reverse mortgages have received bad publicity about aggressive salesmen persuading elderly borrowers to invest in inappropriate products. Indeed, reverse mortgages are not right for everyone. Borrowers should be sure that they want to remain in their home, because they may find themselves with little equity left if they decide to move. They should have a buffer to cover emergencies, because their housing equity will no longer be available. Fortunately, the new regulations are designed to ensure that reverse mortgages are sold only to people who will be able to continue to make their property tax and homeowners insurance premiums. For those who meet these standards, the reverse mortgage can be a very sensible way to increase retirement income.

CONCLUSION

Providing ourselves with adequate retirement income in today's world is hard! But we have levers at our disposal that can lead to better outcomes:

- Working longer provides immediate income; allows us to delay claiming Social Security, which means much higher monthly benefits; provides more time for our 401(k) investments to grow; and shortens the length of retirement.
- 401(k) plans work best if we start contributing early, leave the money in the plan, and rebalance our investments as we age and markets change, use low-fee index funds and target date funds, and are careful about "rolling over" into an IRA.
- In retirement, a couple of sensible strategies can help us draw down our accumulated assets. Annuities—particularly ALDAs—should get serious consideration as a way to spend down at least part of our 401(k) balances. Buying an annuity from Social Security by delaying claiming is also a good idea. For assets that are not annuitized, following the IRS' Required Minimum Distribution rules is a reasonable option.
- Finally, for most households, their home is their major asset and can either be sold or borrowed against to provide additional money in retirement.

The new world of retirement requires more of our attention than the old. But, armed with the right information, we can make choices at every step of our lives that will help us secure a more comfortable retirement.

[5]

WHAT CAN WE DO *AS A NATION*?

Individuals cannot meet the retirement income challenge entirely on their own. We, as a nation, need to take action. We need to make sure that the retirement income system is well structured, with the incentives and products that encourage individuals to make good choices.

Progress is usually made incrementally, so our core proposals build on the system that we already have in place. They include promoting longer work lives, retaining Social Security as a firm foundation of income support, fixing the 401(k) system, rationalizing the favorable tax provisions accorded employer-sponsored plans, and trying to solve the enormous pension coverage problem. But even if all these efforts succeeded, not everyone can work until 70, and many may never have adequate 401(k) holdings. In this case, some people will need to turn to the equity in their home, so downsizing and reverse mortgages should also be encouraged. This agenda may sound like a laundry list, but it is essentially just using our available policy levers to encourage people to work longer and save more.

The advantage of the incremental approach is its reliance on the existing infrastructure rather than trying to build a new system. However, it does assume that a voluntary employer-sponsored pension system is an effective way to provide supplementary retirement income. Some policy experts prefer a fresh start, arguing that only a new structure can effectively provide universal coverage, sufficient saving rates, and improved risk sharing. Two of these "big bang" approaches are also discussed in this chapter.

IMPROVE INCENTIVES TO WORK LONGER

The most potent way out of the box of inadequate retirement income is for us to work longer. Each additional year would have a powerful impact. More working years would enable us to get much higher Social Security benefits, because monthly benefits increase by about 7 to 8 percent for each year we delay claiming. These additional years of work also increase our 401(k) balances because we avoid drawing money now that will be needed later, make new contributions, and earn investment income on this much larger pile of assets. Additional years of work also shorten the period of years over which we must support ourselves in retirement from our 401(k)s. Retiring at 70 rather than 62 changes the ratio of retirement years to working years from 1 to 2 (20 retirement years to 40 working years) to 1 to 4 (12 retirement years to 48 working years).

Social Security's Real Retirement Age Is Now 70

While few know it, 70 is actually Social Security's real retirement age now. The simple fact is that monthly benefits are highest at age 70 and are reduced actuarially for each year they are claimed before age 70. This development is relatively new, which may explain why Social Security's real retirement age is the best-kept secret in town.

But it's time we told everyone. And then we need to clarify what all this talk about raising the so-called Full Retirement Age really means.

Currently workers can claim benefits at any time between 62 and 70. But benefits claimed before age 70 are actuarially reduced to compensate for the fact that they start earlier and will be paid for more years. The policy goal is to ensure that, based on average life expectancy, people who take a lower benefit early receive about the same amount in total benefits over their lifetimes as those who wait to receive higher monthly benefits later.

Most people do not understand how much they increase their benefits by waiting to claim. Benefits claimed at 70 are a full 76 percent higher than benefits claimed at 62. Given that Social Security is a particularly valuable type of income—inflation adjusted and continuing for as long as we live—it makes sense to postpone claiming as long as possible to get the highest monthly amount, assuming we are in good health for our age. An analysis using the National Retirement Risk Index shows that over 85 percent of working-age households would be financially prepared for retirement if they work to age 70 (see figure 5.1).

If 70 is the age at which Social Security pays the highest benefit, what is all this talk about the program's "Full Retirement Age?" It used to be a meaningful concept. Before 1972, maximum monthly Social Security benefits were paid at 65, and monthly benefits were not increased for claiming later.[1] In 1972, Congress introduced a Delayed Retirement Credit, which increased benefits by 1 percent of the Full Retirement Age benefit for each year of delay in claiming. The result was that those who retired later got a small bonus for delaying. But a 1 percent credit did not come close to compensating for the fact that late claimers would get benefits over

Figure 5.1. Working until 70 Does the Trick for Most Retirees
Cumulative Readiness by Retirement Age

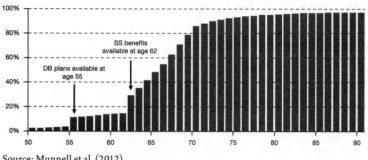

Source: Munnell et al. (2012).

fewer years. In 1983, the adjustment was raised from 1 percent to 3 percent, and then increased gradually to 8 percent by 2008. At this level, the adjustment provided by the Delayed Retirement Credit is actuarially fair—that is, it keeps lifetime benefits constant, on average, for those who claim after the Full Retirement Age. In doing so, the Delayed Retirement Credit has rendered the Full Retirement Age a largely meaningless concept.[2] It does not describe the age when benefits are first available. That is age 62. It does not describe the age when monthly benefits are at their maximum. That is age 70. It really does not have any meaning in terms of an official retirement age.

Is 70 the right retirement age? People are certainly living longer in 2014 than they did in 1940; the increase has been about seven years for both men and women. The question is how these additional years should be divided between work and retirement. One alternative is that the retirement age should keep the expected number of years in retirement unchanged over time, so that all longevity gains are devoted to longer work lives. Another possibility is that the retirement age should keep constant the ratio of the expected years spent in retirement to the expected years working. This seems like a better measure because it distributes gains in life expectancy into both working years and retirement years. Table 5.1 shows that the option of devoting all longevity gains to work suggests a retirement age of 72 in 2020, while the alternative of distributing the gains evenly between work and leisure suggests age 70.

Social Security replacement rates for those with median earnings who claim at age 70 will stabilize around 50 percent (see figure 5.2). But, as discussed earlier, the reported replacement rates overstate the amounts that retirees will actually get in retirement because Medicare premiums are deducted from the gross amount and benefits are subject to the federal income tax.

Table 5.1 70 Is the New 65

Retirement Age Equivalent to Age-65 Retirement in 1940

Year	Age at which	
	Expected retirement years remain constant	*Ratio of expected retirement to working years remains constant*
1940	65	65
1960	67	67
1980	69	68
2000	71	69
2020	72	70

Note: For the ratio of expected retirement to working years, it is assumed that people start work at 20. Expected time in retirement is expected remaining years of life at retirement age.

Source: US Social Security Administration (2004).

Table 5.2 shows that the ultimate "net" Social Security replacement rate at age 70 will equal 43 percent in 2030, very close to the full benefit target established in the 1970s.[3] This replacement rate will provide a solid base on which to add 401(k) savings and home equity for a secure retirement. Those who retire at 62, however, will see net replacement rates of only 24 percent. So retiring at 62 will not be a reasonable option for those who are able to stay in the labor force.

To help Americans make well-informed decisions about when to retire, the Social Security Administration should make clear in

Figure 5.2. Social Security Claimed at 70 Provides a Strong Base
Social Security Replacement Rates for Medium Earner at 62, 65, and 70, by Year Retiree Reaches 65

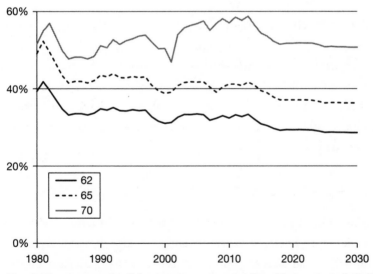

Note: Replacement rates for all three ages incorporate the effect of the increase in the Full Retirement Age from 65 to 66 and the scheduled increase to 67. The age-70 replacement rates reflect the increase in the Delayed Retirement Credit from 3 percent to 8 percent over the period 1983–2008.
Sources: US Social Security Administration (2013b); and Myers (1993).

Table 5.2 Retiring before 70 Means Much Lower Benefits

"Net" Replacement Rate for Medium Worker by Retirement Age, 1980–2030

Claiming age	1980	1990	2000	2010	2020	2030
62	38%	33%	29%	28%	26%	24%
65	48%	42%	37%	38%	34%	31%
70	51%	49%	49%	53%	48%	43%

Note: Year is date retiree reaches age 65. Replacement rate is net of Part B and D premiums, as well as taxation of benefits. Part B SMI deduction for 2030 assumes SMI continues to cover 26 percent of plan costs and uses Trustees' Report enrollment and cost growth assumptions. The assumptions are that the beneficiary has enough other income to have benefits taxed (about $10,000 in 2030) and that the tax rate is 12.5 percent.

Sources: Authors' calculations based on Centers for Medicare and Medicaid Services (2013); and Social Security Administration (2013b).

all of its public communications that age 70 is the program's real retirement age—the age that people should target. Such a shift in the agency's educational efforts—away from the emphasis on the statutory Full Retirement Age—along with a clear explanation of the benefits of working longer would surely have a significant impact over time on the way Americans think about their retirement date.

Increase Social Security's Earliest Eligibility Age

While retiring at 62 is financially undesirable for anyone who can work longer, Social Security currently signals—however unintentionally—that 62 is an appropriate retirement age because it is the Earliest Eligibility Age (EEA) for benefits. This signal is clearly important, as almost 40 percent of participants claim their benefits as soon as they become available. Raising the EEA to, say, 64 would help counter the temptation to claim benefits early and prevent incomes from falling to inadequately low levels later in life.[4]

One problem is that many individuals—perhaps as many as one-third—say they are unable to work past age 62, because they are in poor health, because their jobs are physically too demanding, or because they have lost their jobs and cannot find new work at their advanced age.[5] Many of those unable to work lack the resources to support themselves for those two additional years. To address the needs of this group, one option is to modify existing programs, such as reducing qualification requirements for workers after 62 under Social Security Disability Insurance or lowering the age of eligibility for the means-tested Supplemental Security Income program from 65 to 62. But expanding these programs could be a difficult sell among policymakers concerned about budget deficits. An alternative is to make changes within Social Security for those who cannot work, such as allowing individuals or households with low lifetime earnings to retire earlier.[6]

Another problem is that a higher EEA would reduce lifetime Social Security benefits for low earners and minorities, who have lower-than-average life expectancies.[7] For example, someone who dies at 65 would lose two years of benefits if the EEA were moved from 62 to 64, and that loss would far exceed the higher monthly benefit received between age 64 and 65; in contrast, someone with long life expectancy would more than make up for the two years of foregone benefits by receiving higher monthly benefits over an extended retirement. If such disparities are a concern, raising the EEA should be part of a larger package of reforms that includes provisions that offset such losses to particular groups.[8]

Raising the EEA would not only encourage people to work longer, but could also increase employers' interest in older workers.[9] Many employers think older workers will be on the job only a short time, which taints their view of the productivity of these employees. To the extent that the likely departure date can be pushed out, employers may be more willing to hire, train, and promote older workers. While the perception of older workers as "short-timers" is only one factor affecting employer demand, removing this barrier could cause employers to generally reevaluate their attitude toward workers in their fifties and sixties.

While working longer is a key part of the solution to the retirement income challenge, by itself it will not be enough. Americans, who will need reliable sources of income after they stop working, will need Social Security even more in the future than they have in the past.

MAINTAIN SOCIAL SECURITY

The prediction of a coming retirement crisis—the theme of this book—assumes Social Security continues to pay scheduled benefits. But Social Security is running a long-term deficit. The temptation of many policymakers will be to frame Social Security's deficit as a "budgetary hole that needs to be plugged" and, therefore, to look for a compromise that includes both tax increases and benefit cuts. As discussed earlier, Social Security replacement rates are already declining under current law as a result of previously scheduled benefit cuts, increasing Medicare premiums, and more households with benefits subject to personal income tax. Additional benefit cuts will put more Americans at risk of having inadequate resources in retirement. Cutting benefits is particularly worrisome given that, with the disappearance of defined benefit plans, Social Security will soon be the only source of automatically annuitized benefits for workers in the private sector.[10]

Not changing Social Security benefits at all would require a combined employer-employee tax increase of 2.88 percent to pay benefits for the next 75 years, the planning horizon for Social Security.[11] Is that a feasible tax increase? Interestingly, many did not even notice when Congress cut the employee portion of the payroll tax by two percentage points in 2011 and 2012 and then restored the cut in 2013. From the perspective of the individual, who will see only half of the required increase (the other half is paid—if not borne—by the employer), the tax increase required to eliminate the 75-year deficit is less than the 2013 restoration of the employee rate. So the real question is whether maintaining current benefits and raising the payroll tax makes sense on economic and policy grounds.

Cutting Benefits by Increasing the Full Retirement Age Is Bad Policy

Since 70 is the age at which Social Security pays the full benefit, what does it mean to change the Full Retirement Age? When the Full Retirement Age moves from 66 to 67, as scheduled under current law, benefits for those claiming at any age will be about 7 percent lower, for life. Further increases in the Full Retirement Age have been suggested by various policy experts as a way to help restore solvency to Social Security.[12] But raising the Full Retirement Age to, say, 70 (after we reach 67) would be equivalent to about a 20 percent reduction in benefits. The stated benefit for those claiming at 70 would decline to 41 percent (see table 5.3), and the "net" benefit would be in the 30 percent range. Those levels would no longer be adequate for those

Table 5.3 A Higher "Full Retirement Age" Simply Means a Big Benefit Cut

Social Security Replacement Rates for Medium Earner by Full Retirement Age

Claiming age	Full Retirement Age				
	Current policy		Hypothetical policy		
	66	67	68	69	70
62	31%	29%	26%	24%	22%
65	38%	36%	33%	30%	27%
70	54%	51%	48%	46%	41%

Note: This assumes that Social Security targets a 41.1 percent replacement rate as the replacement rate at the Full Retirement Age. Those who claim at 62 receive 80 percent of what would be received at 65. The Delayed Retirement Credit is 8 percent per year. Early claiming between 62 and the Full Retirement Age is assumed to reduce benefits by 6.67 percent per year.

Source: Authors' calculations and US Social Security Administration (2013b).

working to 70 and would be grossly inadequate for anyone claiming earlier. While some could offset the cut in monthly benefits by working even longer, many could not.[13]

Arguing against increasing the Full Retirement Age is not to say that Social Security benefits can never be cut. People are healthier, better educated, have less physically demanding jobs, and can work longer. They are also living much longer. So keeping monthly benefit levels unchanged results in ever-increasing costs. But the gains in life expectancy have gone mainly to the higher paid, and the discrepancy in life expectancy between high and low earners is getting larger with each cohort (see table 5.4). Cutting benefits using the Full Retirement Age is very hard on those who cannot change their retirement date. If we want to cut benefits, it makes more sense to change the benefit formula directly, which

Table 5.4 Higher Earners Live Much Longer
Age to Which Half of 60 Year Old Males Will Survive, by Birth Year and
Earnings Group

Earnings group	Year of birth			
	1912	1922	1932	1941
Top half	79	81	84	86
Bottom half	77	78	79	80

Note: These data are from a sample of men who had earnings from ages 45 to 55.
Source: Waldron (2007).

allows for larger cuts for the higher paid than for those at the bottom of the earnings distribution.

Given that the Full Retirement Age is now mainly just a budget-cutting mechanism and is largely meaningless for retirement planning, eliminating it would dramatically clarify Social's Security benefit structure. It would clearly signal that claiming at age 70 provides the largest monthly benefit, which would encourage people to work longer. Eliminating the concept would also force policymakers to call a cut a cut, and perhaps target reductions where they would cause less pain.

Solving 75-Year Deficit Not End of Story

With or without some benefit cuts, solving the 75-year funding gap is not the end of the story. Once we reach a steady state where the ratio of retirees to workers stabilizes and costs remain relatively constant as a percentage of payroll, any solution that solves the problem for 75 years will more or less solve the problem permanently. But, currently, we are in a period of transition.

The ratio of retirees to workers will rise from 35 per 100 workers today to nearly 50 per 100 workers in 2035, so the cost rate will continue to rise. Any package of reforms that restores balance only for the next 75 years will show a deficit in the following year, as the 75-year projection period moves forward and picks up a year with a large negative balance. This same pattern of immediate deficits just after a "75-year solution" happened after the last financial fix in 1983.

Policymakers generally recognize the negative effect of picking up deficit years, and many advocate a solution that involves "sustainable solvency," where the ratio of trust fund assets to outlays is either stable or rising in the seventy-sixth year. The problem is that achieving this laudable goal requires larger tax increases or benefit cuts than a 75-year fix.[14]

The issue is one of packaging; full disclosure is necessary so that people don't think the financial fix "failed." People need to know that eliminating the 75-year shortfall is only the first step toward long-run solvency and that a permanent fix for Social Security would require additional changes. And the more that those changes can either be put in the law or at least spelled out in some detail, the more confidence people will have in the financial sustainability of the program.

Consider Investing Part of Trust Fund in Equities

Investing a modest portion of the trust fund in equities could help solve both an economic problem and a political problem.

The economic problem is that Social Security benefits are expensive because, as described in chapter 2, we "gave away" the trust fund in 1939 with the decision to pay benefits far in excess of contributions to early generations of retirees. Equities, with their higher expected return than the bonds currently held in the trust fund, have the potential to reduce required payroll tax contributions.[15]

The political problem is Congress's proclivity to "spend the surpluses." If the Social Security surpluses had really reduced the federal deficit and government borrowing, they would have made more private capital available for private investment, boosting economic growth. But critics claim that Congress thwarted this effort by keeping taxes lower and/or spending more on non–Social Security programs than it would have otherwise.[16] Investment of trust fund assets in corporate equities would make any annual Social Security surplus unavailable to the Congress—the "outlay" to purchase equities would essentially eliminate the surplus—and make it more difficult to use the surpluses to mask deficits in the rest of the budget.[17]

On the other hand, investing the trust fund in equities also requires surmounting some hurdles. First, the financial status of the Social Security program would be calculated assuming risk-adjusted returns from equities, which means that—on paper—equity investing would not improve the financial picture. So the approach would have to be sold on the expectation that, as a practical matter, equity investment would likely generate higher returns and, thus, lower tax burdens. But equities produce those higher returns because they are a more risky investment than the bonds currently held in the trust fund. This risk creates the second hurdle. If realized returns fell persistently short of projections, the government would need to have in place clearly defined procedures for allocating benefit cuts and tax increases over generations.[18] The third hurdle is political.

Some worry about government interference with the allocation of capital in the economy and with corporate activity. This does not seem like a serious problem, however. If half the trust fund balances were invested in equities, even when trust fund balances peak Social Security would hold only about 8 percent of total equities.[19] And the sensible way to invest such funds would be passively managed, low-cost index funds, so "stock picking" would not be an issue.[20]

The question of equity investment is likely to arise again when Congress turns its attention to eliminating Social Security's long-term financing problem, since any immediate increase in taxes will once again produce an increase in trust fund reserves. If these reserves are to increase saving rather than just cover current expenditures, we need a better setup. Investing the Social Security trust fund in equities is worthy of a thoughtful conversation.

Shift Legacy Costs to Personal Income Tax

A little arithmetic quickly shows that current and future workers are paying a lot for their Social Security benefits. If Social Security were financed on a funded basis like 401(k) plans, the average worker would have to contribute less than 10 percent annually to generate a fund adequate to pay benefits equal to 36 percent of earnings.[21] On a pay-as-you-go basis, where no fund is built up and no investment income is earned, a 36 percent replacement rate would require a contribution rate of 18 percent assuming no wage growth.[22] Add in wage growth and the cost rate falls, but remains well above that in a funded system.

We have ended up with a mostly pay-as-you-go system, because, as noted, we gave away to early cohorts the trust fund that otherwise would have accumulated. Many of the early beneficiaries had fought in World War I and had suffered losses in the Great Depression, so the decision to pay benefits far in excess of contributions to those early retirees may have been justified on public policy grounds. But the cost of that decision was to forgo the buildup of a trust fund whose accumulated interest could have covered a substantial part of today's benefits.

The question is whether current and future workers should be asked to pay the higher payroll tax resulting from the decision to give away the trust fund or whether they should be asked to pay simply what they would have to contribute in a funded system. This issue is important because the payroll tax, with no deductions or exemptions, places a significant burden on low-wage workers. One could argue that the legacy burden should be borne by the general population in proportion to the ability to pay—that is, this portion of the Social Security financing problem could be transferred to the personal income tax. Of course, transferring the legacy debt to the personal income tax does not eliminate the burden; the average income tax rate would have to increase by about 4.6 percentage points (from about 19.0 percent to 23.6 percent). Such an increase would be extremely difficult in today's political environment. Nevertheless, the legacy debt must be paid one way or another, and the income tax is a more equitable mechanism than the payroll tax.

FIX THE 401(K) SYSTEM

With a contracting Social Security program, we need to have a first-class employer-based system—one that covers everyone; requires sufficient contribution levels; involves sensible investing;

and provides for an orderly payout of accumulations. Today's 401(k) system, which shifts all the responsibilities to the individual, falls short—far short. We need to make changes to the current system so that it works as well as it can, changes that have already been successfully incorporated in the 401(k) plans of leading companies as best practices and have proven effective.

Improve Participation and Contribution Levels

Two big problems with 401(k) plans are (1) only about 80 percent of eligible participants join the plans; and (2) the median level of combined employer-employee contributions to these plans is only 9 percent.[23] Both these statistics could be improved through the universal adoption of automatic provisions—with an opt-out—already in use by many companies. Policymakers moved toward making 401(k) plans more automatic with the Pension Protection Act of 2006, but that legislation only *encouraged*—rather than *mandated*—adoption of automatic provisions. As a result, less than 50 percent of 401(k) plans have automatic enrollment, and in most cases this feature is applied only to new entrants—not the entire workforce—so the impact is quite limited. Moreover, only 40 percent of those with auto-enrollment also have automatic escalation in the default deferral rate.[24] Without automatic escalation, inertia tends to lock people who are defaulted into the plan into low contribution rates.

To make 401(k)s work better for more participants, we wish that all companies would adopt automatic provisions voluntarily (see box 5.1). But, given experience to date, we think the time may have come to change the law to require all 401(k) plans to adopt auto-enrollment for their entire workforce, with deferral rates set at a meaningful initial level and with annual auto-escalation in

Box 5.1 what companies should do

If most companies with 401(k)s adopt the following best practices, most of their workers would be able to look forward to financially secure retirements.

1. Participation in the 401(k) plan is automatic, with ability for employee to opt out.
2. The default contribution set at a meaningful level with a 50 percent match.
3. In each succeeding year, the company increases the contribution rate of those defaulted into the plan until the combined employee-employer contribution equals 12 percent of pay.
4. Investments are a "target date" managed portfolio of low cost index funds.
5. These practices should be applied to *all* employees, not just to new hires.
6. "Leakages" through hardship withdrawals and loans should be significantly reduced.
7. Separating employees should be encouraged to keep assets with either old or new employer's 401(k).
8. Add an ALDA annuity to reduce the risk of participants out-living savings.
9. Make sure all workers understand the considerable advantages of retiring later.

Many of these best practices were explicitly recommended eight long years ago in the Pension Protection Act of 2006, but most companies have not yet taken action. Fairness has long been a central part of our nation's policies on retirement funds and our nation 'invests' $162 billion in tax benefits each year. So, workers covered by 401(k) plans should know that they will end up with meaningful benefits. If companies are not willing to take action voluntarily, we believe that the auto-401(k) policies should be made mandatory.

the deferral rate.[25] The "back of the envelope" exercise reported in chapter 4 shows that the combined contribution rate should be 12 percent—assuming workers start saving when they are young—if they are going to maintain their standard of living after they stop working.[26] We could achieve this goal if, for example, workers were defaulted into the plan at a deferral rate of 6 percent, their rate increased to 8 percent over two years, and employers matched employee contributions 50 cents on the dollar to add another 4 percent of compensation.[27]

Keep the Money in the Plan

The only way for individuals to retire with sufficient accumulations is to put the money into the 401(k) account and keep it there. Currently a large amount leaks out from both 401(k) plans and IRAs through cashouts at job change and in-service hardship withdrawals, and some leakage occurs through withdrawals at age 59½ and loan defaults. [28] In total, leakages amount to at least 1.5 percent of assets each year, reducing aggregate retirement wealth by more than 20 percent.[29] These leakages, in addition to high investment fees and intermittent plan coverage, are a major reason why the typical household arrives at retirement with only $111,000 in combined 401(k)/IRA savings. We need to change the nature of the current 401(k) system, which is designed both for old-age security and for consumption before retirement, to a system designed exclusively for retirement.

Policymakers face a dilemma in terms of preventing leakages, because studies show that employees who know that they can get access to their funds are more likely to participate and to contribute more once they join the plan.[30] The current provisions therefore reflect an effort to balance the conflicting goals of (1) keeping monies in the plan; and (2) allowing access to those who need their funds to encourage participation and contributions. Thus, the system has a penalty tax and withholding on the one hand and the availability of loans and hardship withdrawals on the other. Even considering this somewhat delicate balance, however, the advantages of access could be structured more efficiently.

It seems like a good time to take a broad perspective that considers all forms of leakages, including withdrawals after age 59½ that occur before a worker retires. Starting from the notion that the goal is to protect *all* retirement saving from leakages, the challenge is to identify circumstances that might warrant exceptions. The most clear-cut case for exceptions would seem to be unexpected financial hardships related to health problems, job loss, or foreclosure, all of which are generally *unpredictable*. In these cases, people should have access to their money, perhaps through a true "hardship loan." Interestingly, it makes little sense to impose a tax penalty on participants just when they are at their most vulnerable.

On the other hand, allowing people access to their tax-supported retirement saving for *predictable* expenses, such as buying a house or paying for college, makes no sense. Participants should not be allowed to borrow or withdraw money for these purposes from either 401(k)s or IRAs. In addition, it is time to raise the age at which withdrawals are allowed without penalty or restriction to coincide with Social Security's Earliest Age of Eligibility, which is currently 62, but we propose moving it to 64. Finally, leakage through cashouts when people change jobs should be closed down entirely.

These proposals that allow access for legitimate reasons eliminate the need for tax penalties. With nonsanctioned access prohibited, sanctioned access should not be penalized. Applying these principles to restructuring access to retirement saving could both provide a safety valve for real emergencies and significantly improve outcomes for today's workers at a time when more saving is needed for a comfortable retirement.

Help Investors Invest Wisely

Putting and keeping money in the plan is only half the battle; the money also needs to be invested well—defined as an appropriate mix of stocks and bonds with low fees. In this respect, government has done two very good things: approving target date funds as a default alternative and improving fee transparency for 401(k)s.[31]

Sanctioning target date funds as a "qualified default investment alternative" solves three problems simultaneously. First, target date funds give individuals an appropriate mix of stocks for the stage in their careers, and rebalances those funds as investors age and as markets change. Second, the underlying assets can be invested in funds with low fees, although this is not always the case. Third, defaulting 401(k) contributions into target date funds precludes overinvestment in the sponsoring company's stock, which is really a bad idea.[32] The percentage of 401(k) participants using target date funds is increasing, albeit slowly. While most people who are automatically enrolled and invested in target date funds stay put, only a fraction of people—usually only new hires—are added each year. As a result, target date funds currently account for only 17 percent of 401(k) assets. This figure will rise, and the increasing use of target date funds will improve overall investment outcomes for participants.[33]

The second positive development is the Department of Labor's 2012 initiative to improve fee transparency. Under the new rules, companies administering 401(k) plans must disclose to the employer all the costs associated with administering the plans.[34] Employers are then responsible for providing participants with expense ratios for investments offered by the plan, showing participants the charges per $1,000 invested. The hope is that when sponsors and participants see the fees, they will respond by moving toward low-cost options, thereby putting downward pressure on expenses.

While these reforms are important, they apply only to 401(k) plans. But the bulk of the money is no longer in 401(k)s; as a result of rollovers from 401(k)s, IRAs have become the biggest form of retirement savings—bigger than 401(k)s. The average individual who rolls over his 401(k) plan into an IRA enters a world in which broker-dealers—who have custody of IRAs—are not currently required to act solely in the best interests of their clients and often have incentives to sell high-fee investments. Given the tax advantages provided to IRAs, as well as to 401(k)s, the government needs to ensure that the accounts are managed in the participants' best interests; high fees frustrate this policy objective. Regulators are currently exploring proposals to make IRAs more responsive to the needs of 401(k) investors, but no changes have yet been made.[35]

Disclosing fees may encourage 401(k) participants to move away from actively managed funds, where expense ratios average well over 100 basis points, over to low-cost index funds, where expense ratios average less than 10 basis points.[36] The investment markets have changed greatly over the past 50 years so that it has become increasingly difficult for active managers to beat the market, particularly when fees are taken into account. As a result, index funds—which continue to gain market share—are widely considered an attractive investment vehicle for a wide variety of asset classes. Some in the investment community might contend that active management would be a better option for narrow market segments, such as emerging markets. But even here, as markets have become institutionalized in recent years, index funds have become a sensible vehicle for investment. The only areas where index funds may not be appropriate are complex categories where research is not widely available, such as high-yield bonds. But individuals saving for retirement probably should not be investing in such assets in the first place. So driving individuals toward index funds for their retirement saving would be an increasingly positive development.

Facilitate Sensible Drawdown

Every 401(k) participant will face the formidable challenge of determining how much to withdraw each year for spending during retirement. Retirees risk either spending their nest egg too quickly or too slowly. These risks could be eliminated through the purchase of either single-premium immediate annuities or Advanced Life Deferred Annuities (ALDAs). But, as discussed in chapter 4, few people purchase either form of annuity.

If either the single-premium annuity or the ALDA is going to gain any traction, we need to take some collective action to make annuities as cheap, safe, and easy as possible. One option is to establish annuities as a default withdrawal mode for some portion of 401(k) balances. Even though the individual can always opt out of the default, this is not a perfect option. Since people often stay where defaulted, the mechanism works best when the default behavior is beneficial for the vast majority of people. While experts agree that almost everyone is better off participating than not participating in a 401(k) plan, it is less clear that everyone is better off with an annuity.[37] But some partial approach should be feasible. One idea would be to make the purchase of an ALDA the default in any withdrawal from a 401(k) plan or an IRA. Another idea would be to make the single-premium annuity the default for half the 401(k) balance or for only the employer's contribution and annuitize the amount slowly—say, over five years—in order to allow people for whom annuities are not the right answer time to halt the process.

The government could also facilitate the provision of annuities—either single premium or ALDAs. At one extreme, the Social Security Administration could allow individuals to purchase (perhaps up to some limit, such as $250,000) larger Social Security benefits, which would be equivalent to the government selling inflation-adjusted annuities. (Such an initiative might stimulate interest in annuities and spur sales in the private sector for wealthier individuals who wanted to annuitize more than $250,000.) Alternatively, the government could specify a standard type of annuity, perhaps including inflation indexing and a maximum load factor, and issue requests for proposals to private sector insurers. If the private insurance companies could satisfy these requirements, the government could serve as a clearinghouse and direct consumers to companies that offered these standard annuities. The government could also act as a purchaser or reinsurer of the approved annuity sold by private companies. The goal would be to establish a public-private partnership that provides 401(k) participants with cost-effective annuities.

If annuities don't gain traction, then people need a simple rule for drawing down their assets. As noted in chapter 4, one recent suggestion is to base withdrawals on the Internal Revenue Service's rules for Required Minimum Distributions (RMD). To promote awareness of this option, the government could consider endorsing the RMD as a guideline.

The important point is that the decumulation phase looms as a potential disaster as baby boomers face the daunting challenge of allocating their 401(k) assets over their retirement years. People need an easy-to-follow withdrawal strategy if they are not going to purchase annuities.

EXPAND COVERAGE

The best practices improvements in 401(k)s described above, and in use now, would make 401(k)s a much more effective alternative to the defined benefit plans that they have replaced. But even the widespread adoption of these suggestions would do nothing for the large number of workers with no employer-based retirement coverage at all.

Only about 50 percent of private sector workers ages 25–64 are covered by an employer retirement plan on their current job.[38] Not having universal coverage means that roughly a third of American households will end up with only Social Security at retirement and that many others will have only minimal 401(k) balances as a result of moving in and out of companies with 401(k)s.

Since most of those without coverage work for small employers without a retirement plan, policymakers have tried to close the gap in the past by introducing simplified products for small businesses. But these initiatives have not improved coverage because plan administration is not the main reason that small businesses do not offer plans. More important considerations for small business are too few employees, lack of employee interest, and unstable business income—concerns that cannot be overcome by streamlining products.

In an effort to improve on past offerings, President Obama recently introduced the MyRA (My Retirement Account). The MyRA has several appealing design features. It recognizes the behavioral reality that many new savers will stop saving if their accounts lose money, so investments in MyRA are limited to a government securities fund until they reach $15,000. It also recognizes the financial reality that small employers have little interest in administering retirement plans, so employers only have to decide to offer the accounts and make payroll deduction available; they have no other administrative role. Finally, the MyRA designers are well aware that small accounts at small employers are very unprofitable to financial services companies, so the Treasury will administer the accounts itself with the assistance of a private sector bank; once account balances reach $15,000, they will be turned over to private sector financial firms to be handled similarly to IRAs. The main drawback to the MyRA is that it is a voluntary program, and past evidence suggests that take-up will be quite limited.

The most effective way to expand pension coverage would involve some type of government requirement that employers offer a plan along with auto-enrollment for their employees (allowing, as with 401(k)s, the ability to opt out). While one option is simply to use the MyRA design coupled with such a requirement, several other proposals have also emerged that would automatically enroll those without coverage and place their contributions in a vehicle outside the employer. No consensus has developed yet over which specific approach would be most effective, but here's a quick look at a few prominent proposals.

- President Obama's "Automatic IRA" would require employers with more than 10 employees to withhold 3 percent of an employee's salary and place it in an IRA.[39] The withheld savings would qualify for a government match through the Saver's Tax Credit.
- Senator Tom Harkin's plan would automatically enroll all workers whose employer does not provide an adequate employer-sponsored plan in a new government-mandated, privately managed defined contribution pension program. The default contribution rate would be 6 percent, contributions would be invested in a commingled portfolio, and payouts from the plan would be in the form of an annuity.[40]
- California's Secure Choice Retirement Savings Trust would deduct 3 percent of pay from the earnings of workers whose employer has no plan, select professional investment managers through a competitive bidding process, and provide a lump sum at retirement.[41] The plan also calls for a minimum guaranteed return product to be purchased in the private sector.[42] The plan is essentially an automatic IRA that would take advantage of the state's infrastructure, but not cost it any money.

The strength of these coverage proposals is that they address a serious problem in the private sector and use the power of auto-enrollment to ensure high levels of participation. The problem with them is twofold. First, they assume that people who are defaulted into coverage will stay there. Second, the contribution levels, which are between 3 percent and 6 percent, do not adequately address the gap between retirement needs and resources.

USE TAX INCENTIVES EFFECTIVELY

The government supports saving in 401(k) plans and IRAs with tax incentives that cost the Treasury $164 billion in 2012.[43] These tax incentives have two problems. First, they give the biggest reward to high earners. If a high earner, with a marginal tax rate of 35 percent, contributes a dollar to a 401(k) plan, he saves 35 cents in income taxes. A middle-income person, with a marginal tax rate of 15 percent, contributing the same amount to his 401(k) saves only 15 cents in income taxes. In terms of simple fairness, it makes no sense to have the size of the incentive depend on earnings. Moreover, the high earner would probably have saved without any tax incentive, while the middle-income earner may well not have.

Second, until recently it has been unclear whether the tax incentives actually encourage people to save more or to simply shift money they would have saved anyway into tax-advantaged accounts. A recent study of Danish data appears to have resolved this question.[44] It found that about 85 percent of people are "passive" savers who pay little attention to tax incentives; they adjust their spending to their take-home pay, and therefore their saving is very responsive to defaults such as auto enrollment. Only 15 percent are "active" savers who would be responsive to tax subsidies; but they respond to subsidies by shifting their money across accounts rather than by altering their total saving. Thus, defaults such as auto enrollment are more effective than tax incentives at increasing saving.

In response to these issues, several policy experts suggest restructuring and/or cutting back on the tax expenditures for retirement plans, such as replacing the current deduction for retirement saving with a credit.[45] Under one proposal, contributions to retirement plans would no longer be tax deductible and instead the government would make a 30 percent matching contribution.[46] As under current law, earnings would continue to accrue tax-free, and withdrawals at retirement would continue to be taxed as regular income. While this proposal would be roughly revenue neutral for the Treasury, it would provide the same matching grant per dollar of saving to low-wage workers as to the higher paid.

The credit approach also provides a simple lever to adjust the magnitude of the subsidy. While 30 percent is revenue neutral at the current level of retirement saving, it would result in an increase in costs if retirement saving were to increase substantially under the 401(k) reforms discussed above. Revenues might also be required to subsidize the savings of low-income workers brought in through an expansion of coverage. Therefore, setting the credit at, say, 15 percent would provide middle-income workers roughly what they receive today, while freeing up tax expenditures for new saving and low-wage workers.

MAKE IT EASIER TO TAP HOME EQUITY

Many of us will need to tap our home equity to maintain our standard of living in retirement. The government has recognized the need for access to home equity by establishing the Home Equity Conversion Mortgage (HECM) program in 1989.[47] Under this program, the government designs the product and provides insurance (for a fee) for the borrower against the risk that the lender can no longer make the contracted payments and for the seller against the risk that the loan balance exceeds the property value. The product is then sold through banks in the private sector. Although the initiative was supposed to be only a demonstration project, HECM loans still constitute over 90 percent of the reverse mortgage market.

Reverse mortgages should be commonplace, but only about 2 percent of possible participants actually opt for such a loan.[48] The government has recently revamped the HECM to both strengthen the program's finances, which had been battered by the financial crisis, and to ensure that those who take out a loan have sufficient reserves to cover property taxes and homeowners insurance premiums. With the program now on a solid financial footing with a restructured product, the government needs to help educate people about the value of their house as a source of income in retirement and clarify that home equity can be accessed either by moving to a cheaper home or by taking out a reverse mortgage.

In addition, the private sector should be encouraged to develop proprietary products for those homeowners whose needs may not be well met by the HECM product. Many people are going to need their home equity in retirement; let's make it easier to tap.

"BIG BANG" ALTERNATIVES

The incremental approach to expanding our retirement saving described above has an important advantage: it relies on the existing system, likely making change easier and more palatable to individuals, employers, and policymakers. But our retirement saving system has evolved over time in a patchwork fashion and does not represent anyone's ideal. As a result, various policy experts have proposed shifting to new plans. The two types of "big bang" alternatives discussed here are a homegrown approach to retirement saving accounts and Australia's "Superannuation Guarantee" program.[49]

The homegrown proposals have many common features. In contrast to the incremental approach, they would establish a single universal savings account rather than relying on an improved 401(k) system plus a separate solution for the uncovered. Coverage could be either mandatory or rely on auto-enrollment to achieve high participation rates. The proposals would reduce investment risk and fees by pooling contributions, using professional investment managers to make decisions, and reducing the riskiness associated with investment returns.[50] Finally, the proposals would provide a reliable stream of retirement income through annuities.

Other policy experts point to Australia's "Superannuation Guarantee" program as a potential model. This program, created in 1992, requires employers to contribute 9 percent of earnings—rising to 12 percent by 2022—to a retirement savings account for each employee. Advantages of this approach include mandatory, universal coverage and reasonable contribution rates. Having the employer make the full contribution also clarifies that the savings are for retirement, which helps reduce leakages. However, unlike the homegrown proposals, Australia allows individuals to allocate their own investments and does not require any annuitization. Another caveat is that some delicacy would be required in transplanting the Superannuation accounts to the United States, because Australia does not have a universal, earnings-related Social Security system as its core source of retirement income; instead it provides means-tested, flat benefits.

One interesting commonality among the "big bang" proposals is that they involve a reduced role for the employer. Such a shift was suggested in 2007 by the ERISA Industry Committee (a membership group for large employers with pension plans) and in 2014 by the American Academy of Actuaries.[51] Many employers feel burdened by the fiduciary and administrative responsibilities of plan sponsorship; they cite complex regulations, escalating costs, and the diversion of their attention away from their main business activities.[52] Under these proposals, the employers' responsibility would be reduced to transferring money to a third-party platform, which would sponsor and administer the retirement plan. Employers would still determine benefit levels, allowing them to compete for workers based on benefit generosity.[53] Reducing the employers' role could solve three problems. One problem is coverage. Currently, only about half of private sector workers are covered by any plan. The uncovered could be defaulted into plans run by the third-party entities. The second problem is leakages. 401(k) balances could remain with the third party when workers change jobs, eliminating cashouts. The third problem is costs. Third-party administration offers economies that could reduce costs for small and midsized firms; it could also lead to more standardized plan design and fee disclosures.

CONCLUSION

The specific proposals discussed in this chapter can seem complicated, but the main message is simple. Those who can work longer should. Nearly everyone needs to save more. As a nation, we should encourage both activities.

Individuals should be made aware that 70 is the age at which they receive maximum Social Security benefits, and retiring earlier significantly reduces monthly benefits. Since most people only save successfully through organized savings mechanisms, we should maintain current Social Security benefit levels *and* make the 401(k) system work better by requiring that all employers adopt automatic provisions *and* expand coverage. If a fresh start were preferred to incremental changes, numerous ideas are out there for a new system of universal retirement savings accounts. Paying off one's mortgage is also an effective way to save, so we need to make sure people recognize that they could use their home equity in retirement and have a way to access that money.

That's the story. We know the steps that we need to take, so let's get started before it's too late for millions of American workers and their families.

NOTES

Chapter 1

1. The average retirement age is the age at which half the population is no longer in the workforce.
2. Traditional defined benefit pensions are still the dominant form of retirement plan for state and local government workers. These public plans have received considerable attention recently due to funding challenges, and their story is important and interesting. However, since public sector workers are only a small minority of the US workforce, their pension situation is outside the scope of this book. For a comprehensive overview of public plans, see Munnell (2012).
3. Amounts for younger age groups are also commensurately lower.

Chapter 2

1. Much of the historical background comes out of conversations with or earlier work by Steven Sass, primarily Sass (1997) and from our joint work (Munnell and Sass 2008). See also Costa (1998).
2. A 1570 census of the poor in Norwich, England, thus found three widows, age 74, 79, and 82, "almost past work" but still earning a small income from spinning. Estates left by the elderly in colonial America often included tools used in less strenuous trades, such as tailoring, spinning, shoemaking, and weaving.
3. Thane (2000).

4. The Census measured the gainful employment rate until 1940 and then the labor force participation rate, defined as the percentage of the population working or actively looking for work.
5. US Census Bureau (1960); Sass (1997); Thane (2000).
6. For an extensive description of the evolution of retirement, see Costa (1998).
7. Veterans eligible for these pensions had significantly higher retirement rates than the population at large (Costa 1998).
8. For an in-depth look at the evolution of the US retirement system, see Schieber (2012).
9. In 1875 American Express set up the first pension plan to provide disability benefits to workers with 20 years of service. In 1880 the Baltimore and Ohio Railroad, noted for its enlightened labor policies, organized a plan based on employee contributions. In 1900 the Pennsylvania Railroad established a plan financed by the employer, which served as a model for other railways. By the end of the 1920s the railway industry had extended pension coverage to 80 percent of its workers. In addition, most large banks, utility, mining, and petroleum companies, as well as a sprinkling of manufacturers, had formal plans.
10. Under most of the early trade union plans, benefits were offered as gratuities and depended largely on the state of the union treasury and its ability to assess members. The first union plan to offer benefits as a matter of right was established by the Brotherhood of Locomotive Engineers in 1912. By 1928 about 40 percent of union members belonged to unions that offered some form of old-age and disability benefits.
11. Some experts also contend that the desire to remove older workers from the labor force was another motivating factor, but DeWitt (1999) makes a persuasive case against such a motivation. The gradual shift in other countries from assistance to social insurance programs strongly influenced the views of the Committee on Economic Security created in 1934 by President Roosevelt; see Witte (1962), Schottland (1963), and Altmeyer (1966). The Committee finally recommended both old-age insurance and old-age assistance programs for the United States, but clearly intended that the insurance program should eventually meet the needs of most of the aged (Pechman, Aaron, and Taussig 1968).
12. From the beginning, however, the benefit formula was progressive, replacing a higher percentage of earnings for the low paid than for the high paid.
13. *Inland Steel Co. v. National Labor Relations Board*, 170 F. 2d at 247, 251 (1949).
14. The government also provides tax incentives for saving for the self-employed and individuals themselves through Keogh plans and Individual Retirement Accounts, respectively.
15. The conventional and Roth 401(k)s offer equivalent tax benefits. Unfortunately, the easiest way to demonstrate this point is with equations. Assume that t is the individual's marginal tax rate and r is the annual return

on the assets in the 401(k). If an individual contributes \$1,000 to a conventional 401(k), then after n years, the 401(k) would have grown to \$1,000 $(1 + r)^n$. When the individual withdraws the accumulated funds, both the original contribution and the accumulated earnings are taxable. Thus, the after-tax value of the 401(k) in retirement is \$1,000 $(1 + r)^n$ $(1 - t)$. Now consider a Roth 401(k). The individual pays tax on the original contribution, so he puts $(1 - t)$ \$1,000 into the account. (After n years, these after-tax proceeds would have grown to $(1 - t)$ \$1,000 $(1 + r)^n$. Since the proceeds are not subject to any further tax, the after-tax amounts under the Roth and conventional plans are identical, assuming that the tax rate that people face in retirement is the same as that when they are young. That is, the deferral of tax on the original contribution and investment earnings is equivalent to exempting the investment earnings from taxation.

16. US Office of Management and Budget (2013a), table 16-4. These provisions, which permit tax deferral on both contributions and the earnings on those contributions, are equivalent to exempting from taxation the earnings on the money that would have been invested after tax, assuming the employee remains in the same tax bracket.

17. The source for the income tax comparison is authors' calculations from US Office of Management and Budget (2013a, 2013b). The military spending comparison comes directly from US Office of Management and Budget (2013b).

18. Ball (1978).

19. US Social Security Administration (2013a). The original exclusion of farm and domestic workers was due to concerns over administrative feasibility of tax collection. Some scholars have indicated a racial motive as well, as blacks were disproportionately represented in these groups. However, a careful study found that such motives—while clearly present—were not responsible for the exclusion (DeWitt 2010).

20. Unfortunately, the indexing procedure contained a technical flaw that caused replacement rates to soar, and this flaw was not corrected until 1977.

21. Martin and Weaver (2005).

22. These data, the most recently available, are from 2004 (Centers for Medicare and Medicaid Services 2007).

23. Kaiser Family Foundation (2011).

24. Nyce and Quade (2012). This study provided data only through 2010 (52 percent); the 2012 figure was estimated from the 2012 Health and Retirement Study, using the 2010 weights.

25. Munnell and Sundén (2004).

26. These numbers come from the Department of Labor's Form 5500. See Buessing and Soto (2006).

27. Munnell and Soto (2007); Rauh and Stefanescu (2009).

28. Munnell and Sundén (2004).
29. The following describes the conventional 401(k). Under a Roth 401(k), the individual contributes after-tax dollars, pays no tax on accruing interest, and takes the money out tax free. The employer's contribution in a Roth 401(k) is treated like a contribution to a conventional 401(k), which avoids the employee having to pay tax when the contribution is made.
30. For data on distribution options offered by employers, see Plan Sponsor Council of America (2013).
31. Kaiser/Hewitt (2005).
32. The span of 75 years was selected because it reflects the maximum number of years a worker is likely covered by the program.
33. US Social Security Administration (2014).
34. Any cut in benefits will come on top of the reduction in benefits associated with the extension of the Full Retirement Age to 67.
35. Kaiser Family Foundation (2011).
36. If these cuts are enacted, then retirees face the risk that many physicians may find it necessary to stop taking Medicare patients.
37. Centers for Medicare and Medicaid Services (2014).
38. Proposals include Ryan (2011) and Domenici and Rivlin (2010).

Chapter 3

1. Technically, the goal is to maximize the expected discounted value of lifetime utility, which requires the individual to smooth the marginal utility of consumption over his lifetime.
2. The replacement rates used in our analysis are derived from a model in which people smooth consumption over their lifetime. Technically, under the life cycle model, people attempt to smooth the marginal utility of their consumption, which varies with many factors, such as age, household size, and health status. But, both in theory and in practice, it is very difficult to determine how much people should save based on smoothing marginal utility. Thus, our replacement rates represent an average rather than a household-specific replacement rate based on marginal utility.
3. While analysts all cite the same factors to explain why retirees need less than their full preretirement income, they employ different approaches to calculating precisely how much less. The RETIRE Project at Georgia State University has been calculating required replacement rates for decades (Palmer 2008). For an array of preretirement earnings levels, they calculate federal, state, and local income taxes and Social Security taxes before and after retirement. They also use the Bureau of Labor Statistics Consumer Expenditure Survey to estimate savings and expenditures for different earnings levels. These

calculations suggest that a couple with an income of $50,000—about our national average—needs 81 percent of preretirement earnings to maintain the same level of consumption. We chose a slightly lower target of 75 percent for a medium earner, in order to err on the side of more conservative estimates. The RETIRE Project calculations also suggest that the required replacement rate varies with income because those with lower incomes save little before retirement and pay little in taxes either before or after retirement.

4. The average retirement age is defined as the age (in years and months) at which the labor force participation rate drops below 50 percent. This methodology evolved from that of Burtless and Quinn (2002), who take the youngest age, in years, at which at least half of men have left the labor force. They calculate the labor force participation rate by age and average over two-year periods (i.e., 1962 and 1963). Our calculations differ in that the results are annual and interpolated to calculate the age in terms of years and months.

5. Many of these same incentives also affected the labor force activity of older women, but the picture is complicated because the labor force participation of women—particularly married women—has also been increasing over time.

6. Burtless (2013).

7. Congressional Budget Office (2014).

8. Centers for Medicare and Medicaid Services (2013); US Social Security Administration (2013b).

9. Webb and Zhivan (2010); Fidelity Investments (2013); Fronstin, Salisbury, and VanDerhei (2012).

10. Munnell (2014).

11. Bricker et al. (2014).

12. Venti and Wise (1989, 1990, 1991, 2001, 2004).

13. The Part B estimates are based on Centers for Medicare and Medicaid Services (2013) and US Social Security Administration (2013b). Medicare Part D premiums are not included in this example as they only began in 2006.

14. Penner (2011).

15. Combined income is adjusted gross income as reported on tax forms plus nontaxable interest income plus one-half of Social Security benefits.

16. The taxation thresholds are not indexed for growth in average wages or even for inflation.

17. In 2011, the Social Security Administration's Office of the Actuary estimated that the percentage of workers subject to taxation of benefits was 35 percent in 2011, and that this figure was projected to rise by about one percentage point per year. Note that the full Social Security benefit is considered for tax purposes even though the Medicare Part B premium is deducted *before* payment.

18. These figures do not include Medicare Part D premiums, as the program did not exist before 2006.

19. Of course, the dollar amount of a two-earner couple's Social Security benefit may be greater, depending on whether the wife earns enough to generate a worker benefit that exceeds the spousal benefit.
20. In the 26 years between 1983 and 2009, Social Security ran cash flow surpluses and built up trillions of dollars of trust fund assets. These trust fund reserves are included in the deficit calculation. The deficit also includes an amount required to bring the trust fund to 100 percent of annual cost by the end of the period.
21. US Social Security Administration (2014).
22. Hacker (2008).
23. Lusardi and Mitchell (2011), cited by Thaler (2013).
24. For examples, see Madrian and Shea (2001), Choi, Laibson, and Madrian (2004), and Mitchell and Utkus (2006).
25. Prior to the PPA, one obstacle for employers was state laws that required employers to obtain an employee's permission before making payroll deductions. The Pension Protection Act amended the Employee Retirement Income Security Act of 1974 to preempt state laws that conflict with automatic enrollment provisions.
26. The government changed the rules in 1998 to allow firms to require workers to "opt out" of a plan, instead of the traditional requirement to "opt in."
27. Nessmith, Utkus, and Young (2007); Fidelity Investments (2007); Madrian and Shea (2001).
28. Choi et al. (2004).
29. To qualify for the safe harbor, the plan sponsor must enroll employees at a deferral rate of at least 3 percent of compensation, increase the employee's deferral percentage over time, and provide either (1) matching contributions for the non-highly compensated of 100 percent on the first 1 percent of contribution and 50 percent on the next 5 percent for a total match of 3.5 percent; or (2) nonelective contributions of 3 percent regardless of whether an employee participates.
30. Nessmith, Utkus, and Young (2007).
31. Plan Sponsor Council of America (2013).
32. In addition to addressing the problem of low saving rates due to inertia, automatic escalation also helps increase future saving among individuals who may find it difficult to save more out of their current incomes. For example, see Thaler and Benartzi (2004).
33. Plan Sponsor Council of America (2013). Vanguard data for the prevalence of automatic provisions show a somewhat different picture, with 32 percent of plans offering auto-enrollment and 69 percent of these plans having an auto-escalation feature (Vanguard 2013).
34. For a discussion of inefficient investment behavior, see Tang et al. (2010).
35. Vanguard (2013/14).

36. Munnell (2014).
37. See Munnell, Orlova, and Webb (2012) for the impact of early saving.
38. One question is how many workers contribute the maximum. Maximum has to be defined because it is not reasonable to think that a person earning $25,000 could contribute $17,500. The definition used here is that the maximum is the lower of $17,500 ($23,000 if over 50) or 25 percent of salary.
39. The good news is that 72.5 percent contribute enough to maximize their employer match. See Aon Hewitt (2013).
40. For data on participant investment in company stock, see Vanguard (2013/14). For a discussion of the problems associated with investing in employer stock, see Benartzi et al. (2007).
41. See Munnell, Webb, and Bleckman (2014 forthcoming) for a detailed discussion of leakage estimates.
42. The source for this figure is the Federal Reserve's Survey of Consumer Finances (SCF), considered the "gold standard" for data on household wealth.
43. The exact definition includes essentially all pretax income that comes into a household in a given year: wages, earnings from self-employment, investment income, interest and dividend income, capital gains or losses, unemployment payments, alimony, welfare, pension income, and some other less common incomes.
44. In constructing the Index, the first step is to project replacement rates for each working household in the Federal Reserve Board's Survey of Consumer Finances. Retirement income at age 65 is defined to include all the usual suspects plus income from taking out a reverse mortgage on the home. This replacement rate is then compared to a target rate that would allow the household to maintain its preretirement standard of living in retirement. If the projected replacement rate is more than 10 percent below the target, then the household is considered "at risk." The Index is simply the percentage of all households that fall more than 10 percent short of the target replacement rate.
45. Scholz, Seshadri, and Khitatrakun (2006); and Scholz and Seshadri (2007). Other researchers also suggest that retirees are likely to have adequate saving. Hurd and Rohwedder (2013) find only modest declines in total spending after retirement. It appears though, that the households they study cannot sustain their initial level of consumption throughout the retirement period.
46. See Munnell, Rutledge, and Webb (2014 forthcoming) for a thorough discussion of the conflicting studies.
47. Coe and Webb (2010).

Chapter 4

1. For a comprehensive discussion of the opportunities and challenges associated with working longer, see Munnell and Sass (2008).
2. In theory, working longer and delaying claiming Social Security are separate issues, but in practice the vast majority of workers claim benefits when they retire.
3. In the case of the spouse's benefit, assuming both husband and wife are collecting benefits, the wife is guaranteed at least half of the husband's full benefit. It doesn't matter when the husband retires; even if his benefit is reduced for early retirement, the wife's benefit is based on the unreduced amount. The spousal benefit *is* reduced if *it* is claimed early.
4. The legal impediment to continued employment—mandatory retirement—was eliminated in 1986 for the majority of workers. In addition, the Age Discrimination in Employment Act of 1967 protects both employees and job applicants who are 40 years of age or older from employment discrimination based on age.
5. The discrepancies were greatest in the following areas: willingness to be flexible about doing different tasks; willingness to participate in training and retraining programs; willingness to try new approaches to problems; willingness to learn and use new technology; and understanding of new technology (AARP 2005).
6. For example, see Helman et al. (2014).
7. Johnson and Kawachi (2007).
8. Helman et al. (2014). Similarly, in a survey of 10,000 workers in a single firm (Choi et al. 2002), 68 percent responded that their saving was too low; they should be saving 14 percent but were only saving 6 percent.
9. For a discussion of the benefits of integrating behavioral economics into the design of the financial system, see Shiller (2012).
10. See Laibson, Repetto, and Tobacman (1998).
11. Thaler and Shefrin (1981).
12. See, for example, Tversky and Shafir (1992) and Iyengar and Lepper (2000). In the economics literature, Iyengar, Huberman, and Jiang (2004) document a strong negative relationship between the number of funds offered in a 401(k) plan and the 401(k) participation rate: having an additional 10 funds in the plan menu reduces the participation rate by 1.5 to 2.0 percentage points.
13. Thaler and Benartzi (2004).
14. US Department of Education (2012).
15. Those who retire earlier would withdraw somewhat less and those who retire later somewhat more. Another option would be to purchase an inflation-indexed annuity, which yields very similar results.

16. Moving from a 4 percent to a 5 percent drawdown strategy would reduce required savings rates and balances by about 20 percent. It would also increase the chances of running out of money from about 5 percent to about 20 percent. Thus, the higher drawdown strategy would require some adjustments over time if returns came in on the low side. Some investment experts have suggested using drawdown rates that are lower than 4 percent; a lower drawdown rate would *raise* required saving rates and balances.

17. The target of 75 percent and the saving rates required are clearly suboptimal for late starters. These individuals would have to impoverish themselves while working in order to achieve a 75 percent replacement rate in retirement, where the income would far exceed their after-savings income before retirement. Moreover, the investment returns are assumed to be fixed; if investment returns were uncertain, people would optimally choose to save more to hedge that uncertainty.

18. The replacement rate is assumed to be slightly lower for the maximum earner—70 percent instead of 75 percent.

19. The calculations assume that the individual earns these amounts throughout his life. Realistically, high earners do not achieve those high earnings immediately on entry to the labor force.

20. Once in retirement, theory suggests that equity allocations should remain constant. In contrast, the nonequity allocation (the mix of bonds and short-term deposits) should change over time so that the average duration reflects the retiree's remaining life expectancy.

21. See, for example, Ellis (2013), Malkiel and Ellis (2010), Malkiel (2005), and Malkiel (1995).

22. Investors could be provided with much more useful information on fees. All fees should be shown together, and fees should be shown *not* as a percentage of assets, or even as a percentage of returns, but as a percentage of incremental returns over the appropriate market index. While certain to be resisted by the investment industry—because the information would be so very disconcerting—this requirement would fit with our traditional public policy emphasis on disclosure to investors of important information.

23. Malkiel and Ellis (2010), worried by this reality, wrote a two-hour guide on investment basics for individuals, *Elements of Investing*. While well over 100,000 copies were bought (and, hopefully, read) that still leaves many millions who have not been taken through the basics. And a meta-analysis of the effectiveness of financial education concluded that most general financial education was ineffective (Fernandes, Lynch, and Netemeyer 2014).

24. For more details on long-term investing strategies, see Taft, Ellis, and Bogle (2012), Ellis and Vertin (1997), and Ellis (2005).

25. In addition, plan distributions between \$1,000 and \$5,000 are generally rolled over automatically to an IRA, unless the participant elects otherwise.

26. A key policy question is whether "leakages" from 401(k)s are big or small. A new study (Munnell, Webb, and Bleckman 2014 forthcoming), which includes a review of the relevant literature, estimates that, overall, leakages reduced final balances in 401(k)s and IRAs by more than 20 percent.

27. Vanguard (2013/14).

28. Munnell and Sundén (2004).

29. Munnell and Sundén (2004); Ameriks and Zeldes (2001).

30. Some may be attracted by the chance to consolidate a number of 401(k) accounts or by a wider menu of investment options.

31. Charles Schwab shows a man with a 1980s boom box and a tag line "Let's talk about that 401(k) that you picked up back in the '80s." Merrill Edge (launched by Bank of America, owner of Merrill Lynch) depicts a woman with her arms spread and the phrase "Catching up with my old 401(k)s." TDAmeritrade shows a sad young woman with writing in the background that says, "roll over your old 401(k)."

32. The simplest annuity is the single-life, single-premium immediate annuity, which involves a one-time payment from the individual, and payments to the individual begin immediately. Other options are also available. Annuities can cover both the husband and wife (joint and survivor), they can provide payments based on some underlying portfolio (inflation indexed or linked to stocks), or they can guarantee payments for a certain period, such as 10 or 20 years. Or they can begin at a later date (deferred).

33. Yaari (1964).

34. The market for variable annuities is actually very large. But these products have historically been sold on the basis of providing tax advantages during the saving accumulation phase. Because very few purchasers convert the balances in these plans to a life annuity at retirement, the growth in this market has not been viewed as a useful measure of the demand for insurance against longevity risk. That demand is usually measured by the purchase of single-premium immediate annuities. This market is only a fraction of the size of the variable annuity market (Brown 2009).

35. Moreover, some advisors may not suggest annuities because the product deprives them of ongoing management fees.

36. Milevsky (2005).

37. Metlife, Inc. (2011).

38. The numbers in these examples are based on industry quotes and authors' calculations.

39. Sass (2012); Shoven and Slavov (2012).

40. The benefit will actually continue as long as you or your spouse is alive if your spouse's benefit is lower than yours.
41. An actuarially fair annuity is one where the present discounted value of the stream of payments to someone with average life expectancy is equal to the premium paid. See Mitchell et al. (1999).
42. Sun and Webb (2012).
43. A Google search for "4 percent rule" and "retirement" produced more than 100,000 hits. Also see Bengen (1994).
44. Failure to take the Required Minimum Distributions results in a 50 percent tax on the required withdrawal amount.
45. See Sun and Webb (2012) for a "horse race" comparison of the performance of different drawdown strategies.
46. The percentages in the RMD tables equal 100 divided by the life expectancy of a couple in which one spouse is 10 years younger. To illustrate, the life expectancy of a couple aged 70 and 60 is 27.4 years. So the RMD for a 70-year-old is 100/27.4 or 3.65 percent. The IRS makes no claim that the tables yield optimal drawdowns; they are simply an ad hoc device to ensure that retirement savings are eventually taxed. Sun and Webb (2012) concludes that the RMD withdrawal rate is a bit on the low side. Households will generally be better off spending the RMD percentages of capital, plus interest and dividends on top.
47. Only 4 percent of households with a death and 11 percent of those with a nursing home entrant sell their house by the next wave of the Health and Retirement Study, which is two years later. See Venti and Wise (2004).
48. Consumer Reports (2012).
49. Interestingly, the same issues have arisen in the United Kingdom. People with very low asset holdings are protected from long-term care expenses; but people over that level have no way to protect themselves from large out-of-pocket expenditures. Private firms do not offer a product because of uncertainty about how long people will live, how much care will cost, and what technical advances might imply. In 2011, the Commission on Funding of Care and Support—called the Dilnot Commission—proposed that the government pay all costs in excess of £35,000. (A pound equals roughly $1.50.) This £35,000 was in addition to a bed-and-board component of £10,000 that individuals were expected to pay out of their pension. The Commission expressed the hope that private firms might enter the market once the government had taken the tail risk off the table. For the poor, the Commission recommended increasing the asset limit from £23,250 to £100,000. As the Commission's proposal weaved its way through the political process, the cap increased substantially. By 2013, the government announced plans to step in once care costs—excluding the bed-and-board component—exceeded £75,000.
50. In addition to ordinary mortgage fees for appraisals, legal fees, and the like, HECMs involve an origination fee to cover the lender's expense and a service

fee to cover the cost of servicing the loan (although this fee is frequently waived). The major expense is mortgage insurance provided by the government to ensure that the borrower gets all the promised payments and the lender is repaid even if the value of the house at repayment is less than the outstanding loan plus interest. The mortgage insurance fee is 2 percent of the home value at closing plus an annual charge of 1.25 percent of the value of the balance outstanding, which is added to the interest rate. See US Department of Housing and Urban Development (2013).

51. The HECM, which provides loans on assessed home values up to the Federal Housing Administration current limit of $625,500, is the most widely used reverse mortgage. Under this program, the government designs the product and provides insurance (for a fee) for the borrower against the risk that the lender can no longer make the contracted payments and for the lender against the risk that the loan balance exceeds the property value. The product is then sold through private sector lenders. The amount available to a homeowner depends on four factors:

1. Home value: the more valuable the home (up to the current cap of $625,500), the larger the loan.
2. Interest rate: the higher the interest rate, the more rapidly the outstanding balance will increase, so the smaller the loan as a proportion of the value of the house.
3. Age of borrower: the older the borrower, the less time for interest to accrue, so the larger the loan.
4. Outstanding mortgage: any proceeds must go first to pay off the existing mortgage, so the larger the mortgage, the smaller the net amount.

52. National Reverse Mortgage Lenders Association (2013).

Chapter 5

1. Interestingly, when 65 was chosen as the program's retirement age back in the 1930s, 70 also received consideration, as roughly half of existing state pension systems used 70 (US Social Security Administration 2013e).
2. This story is not perfect because a number of specific Social Security provisions are linked to the Full Retirement Age. An earnings test applies before the Full Retirement Age but not thereafter. Widow and spousal benefits are reduced if claimed before the Full Retirement Age and not thereafter. Once they reach the FRA, workers can claim spousal benefits and then subsequently claim their own benefits. But all these provisions are relatively small and do not undermine the basic fact that 70 is the age for full monthly benefits under Social Security.

3. The size of the decline in the replacement rate varies somewhat across claiming ages and over time for two main reasons: (1) the phase-in of the higher Full Retirement Age, which varies based on an individual's year of birth; and (2) the taxation of benefits, which occurs above a threshold amount so that those who claim later and receive higher monthly benefits are more likely to be affected.

4. Increasing the EEA has been proposed by a number of policy experts, often in tandem with proposed increases in the Full Retirement Age. One common proposal is a roughly two-year increase in both ages. Since we don't view the Full Retirement Age as a useful concept anymore, we are open to other alternatives for increasing the EEA.

5. Similarly, a survey by Prudential Financial (2005) of a nationally representative sample found that 38 percent of retirees said they had retired *involuntarily*.

6. Initially researchers thought that the EEA could be based on the length of a worker's employment. The intuition is that less educated workers, who enter the labor force at relatively young ages, are most at risk from a rise in the EEA. They disproportionately have physically demanding jobs, which increase the incidence of health problems and make work difficult at older ages; they have relatively poor employment prospects at older ages; and they have relatively low life expectancy. But while less educated workers enter the labor market early, it turns out that they do not have relatively long employment histories because of health impairments and intermittent demand for their labor, resulting in frequent periods of unemployment.

7. And the discrepancy in life expectancy between high and low earners is getting larger with each cohort. See Waldron (2007) and Whitehouse and Zaidi (2008).

8. Raising the EEA does little to improve Social Security's finances since benefits are actuarially adjusted. Those who continue working will contribute some additional payroll taxes, but these amounts are relatively small compared to the size of the financing gap.

9. Several proposals would encourage later retirement. Some, such as making Medicare, rather than the employer, the primary provider of health insurance for those working past 65 and eliminating the payroll tax for those who work more than, say, 40 years, would make older workers cheaper and therefore more desirable to employers. Others, such as increasing the number of years for calculating Social Security benefits, would provide a payoff for continued contributions to the program and encourage people to work longer. These are probably desirable changes, but the single most important reform is the increase in the EEA.

10. State and local government employees are still covered mostly by defined benefit plans.

11. US Social Security Administration (2014).

12. A recent prominent example is the report from the National Commission on Fiscal Responsibility and Reform (2010).

13. Interestingly, those who retire at age 70 cannot replicate their previous monthly benefit by working longer, because the Delayed Retirement Credit is not applicable after 70. No matter what they do, they will see a reduction in their monthly as well as lifetime benefits. Right now, this is not a significant problem. The age-70 retirees today are largely lawyers, doctors, and Ph.D.s, as discussed above. Moreover, if age 70 is considered the "correct" age, it is not necessary to incent people to work longer. But if retirement patterns change and the correct age is deemed to be more than 70, then policymakers will need to consider extending the Delayed Retirement Credit beyond age 70.

14. Diamond and Orszag (2005), for example, explicitly recognize this issue and incorporate such a broader fiscal fix in their recommendations for solving Social Security's financial imbalance.

15. Such an initiative would be especially beneficial for young workers who should take on some risk through equity investment but often do not have the required resources. Investing in equities through the trust fund also allows people to hold their risky assets in a place where gains and losses can be smoothed over time.

16. Smetters (2004). Economists have tried to estimate how the surpluses affected congressional behavior, but the results are not very persuasive. Our best assessment is that, before 2000, the Social Security surpluses added to national saving. After 2000, when the entire budget appeared to be moving toward rising surpluses, the optics made large tax cuts too tempting. In other words, we think that the Social Security surpluses helped enable the so-called Bush tax cuts.

17. Consider the following example. Under the current arrangements in which Social Security invests in government bonds, if Social Security generates a surplus of $100 billion and the rest of the budget generates a deficit of $150 billion, the overall deficit is $50 billion. If Social Security were to invest its $100 billion surplus in equities, however, the outlay associated with purchasing equities would offset the program's surplus and the overall deficit would be $150 billion.

18. Ponds and van Riel (2007).

19. This share is well below the 11 percent currently held by state and local pension plans—a level that does not seem to have raised any concerns. Moreover, with index fund turnover of only 5 percent, trading by such index funds would be less than one-half of 1 percent of stock market trading.

20. Canada invests a portion of the Canadian Pension Plan's assets in private sector investments, and that strategy seems to be working smoothly (Weaver 2004).

21. This calculation assumes the Social Security Trustees' real interest rate of 2.9 percent, and that individuals begin contributing at age 25 and retire at age 65.
22. That is, each of the two workers would pay for half of the retiree's benefit.
23. Munnell (2014); Vanguard (2014).
24. Plan Sponsor Council of America (2013).
25. Industry voices have expressed support for expanded use of fully automatic 401(k)s. For example, see Putnam Investments (2013a, 2013b).
26. The comparable figure for an 80 percent replacement rate would be 14 percent.
27. A recent survey suggests that raising the default deferral rate from 3 percent to 6 percent should cause little disruption. Of a sample of about 1,000 working-age respondents, the percentage saying they would cancel the contribution if the deferral rate rose from 3 percent to 6 percent rose only from 11 percent to 16 percent (Helman et al. 2013).
28. Lu et al. (2014) estimate that default leakage amounts to only $6 billion per year.
29. Munnell, Webb, and Bleckman (2014 forthcoming). The annual leakage estimate is based on a review of several studies, including Bryant, Holden, and Sabelhaus (2011); Argento, Bryant, and Sabelhaus (2013); Vanguard (2013/14); and Butrica, Zedlewski, and Issa (2010).
30. For example, see Munnell, Sundén, and Taylor (2002) and the literature cited therein.
31. Mitchell and Utkus (2012) discuss how the government approval of target date funds as a default for 401(k)s has helped boost the popularity of these funds.
32. It is a bad idea because investing in a single stock rather than an index creates more risk without any additional return and because participants are investing in an asset highly correlated with their own earnings.
33. Vanguard (2014) estimates that, by 2018, 58 percent of all 401(k) participants will be entirely invested in a target date fund or other professionally managed investment option.
34. Plan sponsors are supposed to use this information to ensure that the fees are reasonable. That is, they have to prudently select and monitor their service provider.
35. For example, the Department of Labor has proposed changes that, among other things, would prevent broker-dealers from receiving third-party payments such as 12b-1 fees, which provide an incentive for broker dealers to sell high-fee mutual funds. The prohibition, however, would have only a limited impact on costs to investors.
36. Investment Company Institute (2013). For further discussion on the benefits of low fees, see Malkiel (1995, 2005) and Ellis (2013).

37. Moreover, it is much more difficult to unwind an annuity, since giving people their money back, if, say, they got sick, would undermine the mortality pooling, which produces the mortality premium that makes annuities attractive.

38. Munnell and Bleckman (2014).

39. US Office of Management and Budget (2013c). Employees could choose between a Roth and a traditional IRA, but the Roth, which allows low-income workers who may need the money to withdraw funds without penalty, is the default. Additionally, the proposal provides a tax credit to help small businesses with implementation costs.

40. US Senate Health, Education, Labor and Pensions Committee (2014).

41. California State Legislature (2012). The proposal was adopted in 2012, but has not yet been implemented because the legislation simply authorizes a feasibility study and seeks approval from federal regulators. The US Department of Labor must determine that the California law is not preempted by ERISA and the Internal Revenue Service needs to rule that the contributions to the retirement plan could be made on a pretax basis. The managers could be either private sector firms or the California Public Employees Retirement System (CalPERS). The whole program would be overseen by a seven-person board, consisting of the state treasurer, director of finance, comptroller, and four people appointed by the governor and the legislature.

42. Since private sector firms cannot guarantee more than the riskless rate without enormous expense, the guarantee would be modest.

43. The cost is estimated as the difference between the present value of the revenue forgone, net of the present value of future tax payments, with respect to contributions made in a given year.

44. Chetty et al. (2012).

45. Both the 2010 National Commission on Fiscal Responsibility and Reform (cochaired by Erskine Bowles and Senator Alan Simpson) and the 2010 Bipartisan Policy Center's Debt Reduction Task Force (cochaired by Senator Pete Domenici and Alice Rivlin) recommended consolidating retirement accounts and capping tax-preferred contributions at the lower of $20,000 or 20 percent of income. This change would limit the advantage of 401(k)s for higher earners. On the other hand, both commissions proposed taxing capital gains and dividends as ordinary income, which would increase the value of the favorable tax provisions. In 2014, Representative David Camp put out a blueprint to reform the nation's tax system, which included provisions that would limit the tax benefits for retirement saving to a 25 percent marginal rate (US House of Representatives, Ways and Means Committee 2014).

46. See Gale, Gruber, and Orszag (2008). The 30 percent match would apply for all contributions up to the minimum of either (a) 10 percent of adjusted gross income; or (b) $20,000 for 401(k) accounts and $5,000 for IRAs. These limits would be indexed for inflation.

47. The program is operated by the US Department of Housing and Urban Development. Shan (2009).
48. Nakajima and Telyukova (2013).
49. For examples of homegrown proposals, see Davis and Madland (2013) and Ghilarducci (2008). For a brief summary of the Australian system, see Agnew (2013).
50. Davis and Madland (2013) suggest a "collar" that would constrain annual investment returns credited to the accounts to a range of 0 percent to 8 percent. Ghilarducci (2008) proposes a fixed real rate of return of 3 percent.
51. The ERISA Industry Committee (2007); American Academy of Actuaries (2014).
52. The ERISA Industry Committee (2007).
53. They would have a duty not to lose the employee's money—similar to their responsibility for transferring employees' payroll taxes to Social Security—but beyond that they would be free of fiduciary responsibilities.

BIBLIOGRAPHY

AARP. 2005. *American Business and Older Employees: A Focus on Midwest Employers.* Washington, DC.

Agnew, Julie. 2013. *"Australia's Retirement System: Strengths, Weaknesses, and Reforms."* Issue in Brief 13-5. Chestnut Hill, MA: Center for Retirement Research at Boston College.

Altmeyer, Arthur J. 1966. *The Formative Years of Social Security.* Madison: University of Wisconsin Press.

American Academy of Actuaries. 2014. *"Retirement for the AGES: Building Enduring Retirement-Income Systems."* A Public Policy Monograph. Washington, DC.

Ameriks, John, and Stephen P. Zeldes. 2001. *"How Do Household Portfolio Shares Vary with Age?"* Working Paper 6-120101. New York: TIAA-CREF Research Institute.

Argento, Robert, Victoria L. Bryant, and John Sabelhaus. 2013. "Early Withdrawals from Retirement Accounts during the Great Recession." Finance and Economics Discussion Series 2013-22. Washington, DC: Federal Reserve Board.

Aon Hewitt. 2013. *2013 Universe Benchmarks: Measuring Employees Savings and Investing Behavior in Defined Contribution Plans—Highlights.* Lincolnshire, IL.

Ball, Robert M. 1978. *Social Security Today and Tomorrow.* New York: Columbia University Press.

Bell, Felicitie C. 1997. "*Table 3. Total Fertility Rates by Calendar Year and Alternative.*" Actuarial Study No. 112. Washington, DC: US Social Security Administration.

Benartzi, Shlomo, Richard H. Thaler, Stephen P. Utkus, and Cass R. Sunstein. 2007. "The Law and Economics of Company Stock in 401(k) Plans." *Journal of Law and Economics* 50(1): 45–79.

Bengen, William P. 1994. "Determining Withdrawal Rates Using Historical Data." *Journal of Financial Planning* 7(4): 171–180.

Bricker, Jesse, Lisa J. Dettling, Alice Henriques, Joanne W. Hsu, Kevin B. Moore, John Sabelhaus, Jeffrey Thompson, and Richard A. Windle. 2014. "Changes in U.S. Family Finances from 2010 to 2013: Evidence from the Survey of Consumer Finances." Federal Reserve Bulletin 100(4): 1-41.

Brown, Jeffrey R. 2009. "Financial Education and Annuities." *OECD Journal: General Papers* 2008(3): 173–215.

Bryant, Victoria L., Sarah Holden, and John Sabelhaus. 2011. "*Qualified Retirement Plans: Analysis of Distribution and Rollover Activity.*" WP 2011-01. Philadelphia, PA: Pension Research Council.

Buessing, Marric, and Mauricio Soto. 2006. "*The State of Private Pensions: Current 5500 Data.*" Issue in Brief 42. Chestnut Hill, MA: Center for Retirement Research at Boston College.

Burtless, Gary. 2013. "*The Impact of Population Aging and Delayed Retirement on Workforce Productivity.*" Working Paper 2013-11. Chestnut Hill, MA: Center for Retirement Research at Boston College.

Burtless, Gary, and Joseph F. Quinn. 2002. "*Is Working Longer the Answer for an Aging Workforce?*" Issue in Brief 11. Chestnut Hill, MA: Center for Retirement Research at Boston College.

Butrica, Barbara A., Sheila R. Zedlewski, and Philip Issa. 2010. "*Understanding Early Withdrawals from Retirement Accounts.*" Discussion Paper 10-02. Washington, DC: Urban Institute.

California State Legislature. 2012. "SB 1234: Retirement Savings Plans." Sacramento, CA. Available at http://leginfo.legislature.ca.gov/faces/billStatusClient.xhtml.

Centers for Medicare and Medicaid Services. 2007. "*2004 National Health Expenditures by Age.*" Unpublished data provided by request from the Office of the Actuary, National Health Statistics Group. Washington, DC: Department of Health and Human Services.

———. 2013, 2014. *Annual Report of the Board of Trustees of the Federal Hospital Insurance and Federal Supplementary Medical Insurance Trust Funds.* Washington, DC: Government Printing Office.

Chetty, Raj, John N. Friedman, Soren Leth-Petersen, Torben Nielsen, and Tore Olsen. 2012. "*Active vs. Passive Decisions and Crowdout in Retirement Savings Accounts: Evidence from Denmark.*" Working Paper 18565. Cambridge, MA: National Bureau of Economic Research.

Choi, James J., David Laibson, and Brigitte C. Madrian. 2004. "Plan Design and 401(k) Savings Outcomes." *National Tax Journal* 57(2): 257–298.

Choi, James J., David Laibson, Brigitte C. Madrian, and Andrew Metrick. 2002. "Defined Contribution Pensions: Plan Rules, Participant Decisions, and the Path of Least Resistance." In *Tax Policy and the Economy*, vol. 16, edited by James M. Poterba, 67–113. Cambridge, MA: MIT Press.

———. 2004. "For Better or for Worse: Default Effects and 401(k) Savings Behavior." In *Perspectives on the Economics of Aging*, edited by David A. Wise, 81–126. Chicago: University of Chicago Press.

Coale, Ansley J., and Melvin Zelnick. 1963. *New Estimates of Fertility and Population in the U.S.* Princeton, NJ: Princeton University Press.

Coe, Norma B. and Anthony Webb. 2010. "*Children and Household Utility: Evidence from Kids Flying the Coop.*" Working Paper 2010-16. Chestnut Hill, MA: Center for Retirement Research at Boston College.

Congressional Budget Office. 2014. *The Budget and Economic Outlook: 2014 to 2024.* Washington, DC.

Consumer Reports. 2012. "Long-Term-Care Insurance: Insurers Are Forced to Boost Premiums or Stop Selling Policies." *Consumer Reports Monthly Adviser*, August.

Costa, Dora L. 1998. *The Evolution of Retirement: An American Economic History, 1880–1990.* Chicago: University of Chicago Press.

Davis, Rowland, and David Madland. 2013. *American Retirement Savings Could Be Much Better.* Washington, DC: Center for American Progress.

Diamond, Peter A., and Peter R. Orszag. 2005. *Saving Social Security: A Balanced Approach.* Washington, DC: Brookings Institution Press.

Dewitt, Larry. 1999. "The History and Development of the Social Security Retirement Earnings Income Test." Historian's Office Special Study 7. Washington, DC: Social Security Administration.

———. 2010. "The Decision to Exclude Agricultural and Domestic Workers from the 1935 Social Security Act." *Social Security Bulletin* 70(4): 49–68.

Domenici, Pete, and Alice Rivlin. 2010. *Restoring America's Future: Reviving the Economy, Cutting Spending and Debt, and Creating a Simple, Pro-growth Tax System.* Washington, DC: Bipartisan Policy Center.

Ellis, Charles D. 2005. *Capital: The Story of Long-Term Investment Excellence.* Hoboken, NJ: John Wiley & Sons.

———. 2013. *Winning the Loser's Game: Timeless Strategies for Successful Investing.* Columbus, OH: McGraw-Hill.

Ellis, Charles D., and James R. Vertin. 1997. *The Investor's Anthology: Original Ideas from the Industry's Greatest Minds.* Hoboken, NJ: John Wiley & Sons.

The ERISA Industry Committee. 2007. *A New Benefit Platform for Life Security.* Washington, DC.

Fernandes, Daniel, John G. Lynch Jr., and Richard G. Netemeyer. 2014. "Financial Literacy, Financial Education and Downstream Financial Behaviors." *Management Science*. Published online in Articles in Advance 27 (January).

Fidelity Investments. 2007. *Building Futures. Vol. 8: A Report on Corporate Defined Contribution Plans*. Boston, MA.

———. 2013. "Fidelity Estimates Couples Retiring in 2013 Will Need $220,000 to Pay Medical Expenses Throughout Retirement." May 15.

Fronstin, Paul, Dallas Salisbury, and Jack VanDerhei. 2012. "Savings Needed for Health Expenses for People Eligible for Medicare: Some Rare Good News." *Notes* 33(10): 1–7.

Gale, William G., Jonathan Gruber, and Peter R. Orszag. 2008. "Improving Opportunities and Incentives for Saving by Middle- and Low-Income Households." In *Path to Prosperity: Hamilton Project Ideas on Income Security, Education, and Taxes*, edited by Jason Furman and Jason Bordoff, 93–126. Washington, DC: Brookings Institution.

Ghilarducci, Teresa. 2008. *When I'm Sixty-Four: The Plot against Pensions and the Plan to Save Them*. Princeton, NJ: Princeton University Press.

Hacker, Jacob. 2008. *The Great Risk Shift: The New Economic Insecurity and the Decline of the American Dream*. New York: Oxford University Press.

Haubrich, Joseph G., George Pennacchi, and Peter Ritchken. 2011. "*Inflation Expectations, Real Rates, and Risk Premia: Evidence from Inflation Swaps*." Working Paper 11-07. Cleveland, OH: Federal Reserve Bank of Cleveland.

Health Research and Educational Trust. 2013. *Employer Health Benefits Annual Survey, 2013*. Chicago, IL.

Helman, Ruth, Nevin Adams, Craig Copeland, and Jack VanDerhei. 2013. "*The 2013 Retirement Confidence Survey: Perceived Savings Needs Outpace Reality for Many*." Issue Brief 384. Washington, DC: Employee Benefit Research Institute.

———. 2014. "The 2014 Retirement Confidence Survey: Confidence Rebounds—for Those with Retirement Plans." Issue Brief 397. Washington, DC: Employee Benefit Research Institute.

Hurd, Michael D., and Susann Rohwedder. 2013. "Heterogeneity in Spending Change at Retirement." *Journal of the Economics of Ageing* 1(2): 60–71.

Internal Revenue Service. 2012. "*Individual Retirement Arrangements (IRAs)*." Publication 590. Washington, DC.

Investment Company Institute. 2013. "*2012 Investment Company Fact Book*." Washington, DC.

Iyengar, Sheena S., Gur Huberman, and Wei Jiang. 2004. "How Much Choice Is Too Much? Contributions to 401(k) Retirement Plans." In *Pension Design and Structure: New Lessons from Behavioral Finance*, edited by Olivia S. Mitchell and Stephen P. Utkus, 83–96. New York: Oxford University Press.

Iyengar, Sheena S., and Mark R. Lepper. 2000. "When Choice Is Demotivating: Can One Desire Too Much of a Good Thing?" *Journal of Personality and Social Psychology* 79(6): 995–1006.

Johnson, Richard, and Janette Kawachi. 2007. "*Job Changes at Older Ages: Effects on Wages, Benefits, and Other Job Attributes.*" Working Paper 2007-4. Chestnut Hill, MA: Center for Retirement Research at Boston College.

Kaiser/Hewitt. 2005. *Prospects for Retiree Health Benefits as Medicare Prescription Drug Coverage Begins: Findings from the Kaiser/Hewitt 2005 Survey on Retiree Health Benefits.* Menlo Park, CA and Lincolnshire, IL: Kaiser Family Foundation and Aon Hewitt Associates.

Kaiser Family Foundation. 2011. *Medicare Spending and Financing: A Primer.* Menlo Park, CA.

Laibson, David, Andrea Repetto, and Jeremy Tobacman. 1998. "Self Control and Saving for Retirement." *Brookings Papers on Economic Activity* 1998(1): 91–196.

Lu, Timothy (Jun), Olivia S. Mitchell, Stephen P. Utkus, and Jean A. Young. 2014. "*Borrowing from the Future: 401(k) Plan Loans and Loan Defaults.* Working Paper WP2014-01. Philadelphia, PA: Pension Research Council.

Lusardi, Annamaria, and Olivia S. Mitchell. 2011. "Financial Literacy and Retirement Planning in the United States." *Journal of Pension Economics and Finance* 10(4): 509–525.

Madrian, Brigitte C., and Dennis F. Shea. 2001. "The Power of Suggestion: Inertia in 401(k) Participation and Savings Behavior." *Quarterly Journal of Economics* 116(4): 1149–1187.

Malkiel, Burton G. 1995. "Returns from Investing in Equity Mutual Funds 1971 to 1991." *Journal of Finance* 1(2): 549–572.

———. 2005. "Reflections on the Efficient Market Hypothesis: 30 Years Later." *Financial Review* 40(2005): 1–9.

Malkiel, Burton G., and Charles D. Ellis. 2010. *The Elements of Investing.* Hoboken, NJ: John Wiley & Sons.

Martin, Patricia P., and David A. Weaver. 2005. "Social Security: A Program and Policy History." *Social Security Bulletin* 66(1): 1–15.

Mercer/Australian Center for Financial Studies. 2013. *Melbourne Mercer Global Pension Index.* Melbourne, Australia.

Metlife, Inc. 2011. *Longevity Income Guarantee.* New York, NY.

Milevsky, Moshe A. 2005. "Real Longevity Insurance with a Deductible: Introduction to Advanced-Life Delayed Annuities." *North American Actuarial Journal* 9(4): 109–122.

Mitchell, Olivia S., James Poterba, Mark Warshawsky, and Jeffrey Brown. 1999. "New Evidence on the Money's Worth of Individual Annuities." *American Economic Review* 89(5): 1299–1318.

Mitchell, Olivia S., and Stephen P. Utkus. 2006. "How Behavioral Finance Can Inform Retirement Plan Design." *Journal of Applied Corporate Finance* 18(1): 82–94.

———. 2012. "Target-Date Funds in 401(k) Retirement Plans." Working Paper 17911. Cambridge, MA: National Bureau of Economic Research.

Munnell, Alicia H. 2012. *State and Local Pensions: What Now?* Washington, DC: Brookings Institution Press.

Munnell, Alicia H. 2014. "401(k)/IRA Holdings in 2013: An Update from the SCF." Issue in Brief 14-15. Chestnut Hill, MA: Center for Retirement Research at Boston College.

Munnell, Alicia H., and Dina Bleckman. 2014. *"Is Pension Coverage a Problem in the Private Sector?* Issue in Brief 14-7. Chestnut Hill, MA: Center for Retirement Research at Boston College.

Munnell, Alicia H., Natalia Orlova, and Anthony Webb. 2012. *"How Important Is Asset Allocation to Financial Security in Retirement?"* Working Paper 2012–13. Chestnut Hill, MA: Center for Retirement Research at Boston College.

Munnell, Alicia H., Matthew S. Rutledge, and Anthony Webb. 2014 (forthcoming). *"Are Retirees Falling Short? Reconciling the Conflicting Evidence."* Working Paper. Chestnut Hill, MA: Center for Retirement Research at Boston College.

Munnell, Alicia H., and Steven A. Sass. 2008. *Working Longer: The Solution to the Retirement Income Challenge.* Washington, DC: Brookings Institution Press.

Munnell, Alicia H., and Mauricio Soto. 2007. *"Why Are Companies Freezing Their Pensions?"* Working Paper 2007-22. Chestnut Hill, MA: Center for Retirement Research at Boston College.

Munnell, Alicia H., and Annika Sundén. 2004. *Coming Up Short: The Challenge of 401(k) Plans.* Washington, DC: Brookings Institution Press.

Munnell, Alicia H., Annika Sundén, and Catherine Taylor. 2002. "What Determines 401(k) Participation and Contributions?" *Social Security Bulletin* 64(3): 64–75.

Munnell, Alicia H., Anthony Webb, and Dina Bleckman. 2014 (forthcoming). *"The Impact of Leakages from 401(k)s and IRAs.* Working Paper. Chestnut Hill, MA: Center for Retirement Research at Boston College.

Munnell, Alicia H., Anthony Webb, Luke Delorme, and Francesca Golub-Sass. 2012. *"National Retirement Risk Index: How Much Longer Do We Need to Work?"* Issue in Brief 12-12. Chestnut Hill, MA: Center for Retirement Research at Boston College.

Myers, Robert J. 1993. *Social Security.* 4th ed. Philadelphia: Pension Research Council, University of Pennsylvania Press.

Nakajima, Makoto, and Irina A. Telyukova. 2013. *"Reverse Mortgage Loans: A Quantitative Analysis."* Working Paper 13-27. Philadelphia, PA: Federal Reserve Bank of Philadelphia.

National Commission on Fiscal Responsibility and Reform. 2010. *The Moment of Truth: Commission Report.* Washington, DC: White House.

National Reverse Mortgage Lenders Association. 2013. "Reverse Mortgage Calculator." Available at http://www.reversemortgage.org/About/ReverseMortgageCalculator.aspx.

Nessmith, William E., Stephen P. Utkus, and Jean A. Young. 2007. *Measuring the Effectiveness of Automatic Enrollment.* Valley Forge, PA: Vanguard Center for Retirement Research.

Nyce, Steve, and Billie Jean Quade. 2012. *Annuities and Retirement Happiness.* New York: Towers Watson.

Palmer, Bruce A. 2008. *"2008 GSU/Aon RETIRE Project Report."* Research Report Series 08-1. Atlanta: J. Mack Robinson College of Business, Georgia State University.

Pechman, Joseph A., Henry J. Aaron, and Michael K. Taussig. 1968. *Social Security: Perspectives for Reform.* Washington, DC: Brookings Institution Press.

Penner, Rudolph G. 2011. *"Medicare Premiums and Social Security's Cost-of-Living Adjustments."* Washington, DC: Program on Retirement Policy, Urban Institute.

Plan Sponsor Council of America. 2013. *56th Annual Survey of Profit Sharing and 401(k) Plans.* Chicago, IL.

Ponds, Eduard H. M., and Bart van Riel. 2007. *"The Recent Evolution of Pension Funds in the Netherlands: The Trend to Hybrid DB-DC Plans and Beyond."* Working Paper 2007-9. Chestnut Hill, MA: Center for Retirement Research at Boston College.

Prudential Financial. 2005. *Roadblocks to Retirement: A Report on What Happens When Living Today Gets in the Way of Financial Security Tomorrow.* Prudential's Four Pillars of Retirement Series.

Putnam Investments. 2013a. "Three Steps That Could Shore Up Retirement Security." Retirement Savings Challenge (blog), July 9.

———. 2013b. "Putnam Investments CEO Robert L. Reynolds Calls for Innovations in Product, Portfolio Strategy and Risk Management to Address Investors' Evolving Needs." Press Release, March 12.

Rauh, Joshua D., and Irina Stefanescu. 2009. "Why Are Firms in the United States Abandoning Defined Benefit Plans?" *Rotman International Journal of Pension Management* 2(2): 18–25.

Ryan, Paul. 2011. *The Path to Prosperity: Restoring America's Promise.* Fiscal Year 2012 Budget Resolution. Washington, DC: House Committee on the Budget.

Sass, Steven A. 1997. *The Promise of Private Pensions: The First Hundred Years.* Cambridge, MA: Harvard University Press.

———. 2012. *"Should You Buy an Annuity from Social Security?"* Issue in Brief 12-10. Chestnut Hill, MA: Center for Retirement Research at Boston College.

Schieber, Sylvester. 2012. *The Predictable Surprise: The Unraveling of the U.S. Retirement System*. New York: Oxford University Press.

Scholz, John Karl and Ananth Seshadri. 2008. "Are All Americans Saving 'Optimally' for Retirement?" Presented at the 10th Annual RRC Conference in Washington, DC, August 7–8.

Scholz, John Karl, Ananth Seshadri, and Surachai Khitatrakun. 2006. "Are Americans Saving 'Optimally' for Retirement?" *Journal of Political Economy* 114(4): 607–643.

Schottland, Charles I. 1963. *The Social Security Program in the United States*. New York: Appleton-Century-Crofts.

Shan, Hui. 2009. "Reversing the Trend: The Recent Expansion of the Reverse Mortgage Market." *Finance and Economics Discussion Series* 2009-42. Washington, DC: Federal Reserve Board.

Shiller, Robert J. 2012. *Finance and the Good Society*. Princeton, NJ: Princeton University Press.

Shoven, John B., and Sita Nataraj Slavov. 2012. "*The Decision to Delay Social Security Benefits: Theory and Evidence*." Working Paper 17866. Cambridge, MA: National Bureau of Economic Research.

Skolnik, Alfred. 1976. "Private Pension Plans, 1950–1974." *Social Security Bulletin* 39(6): 3–17.

Smetters, Kent. 2004. "Is the Social Security Trust Fund a Store of Value?" *American Economic Review* 94(2): 176–181.

Sun, Wei, and Anthony Webb. 2012. "*Should Households Base Asset Decumulation Strategies on Required Minimum Distribution Tables?*" Working Paper 2012-10. Chestnut Hill, MA: Center for Retirement Research at Boston College.

Taft, John G., Charles D. Ellis, and John C. Bogle. 2012. *Stewardship: Lessons Learned from the Lost Culture of Wall Street*. Hoboken, NJ: John Wiley & Sons.

Tang, Ning, Olivia S. Mitchell, Gary R. Mottola, and Stephen P. Utkus. 2010. "The Efficiency of Sponsor and Participant Portfolio Choices in 401(k) Plans." *Journal of Public Economics* 94(11–12): 1073–1085.

Thaler, Richard H. 2013. "Financial Literacy, beyond the Classroom." Economic View (op-ed), *New York Times*, October 5.

Thaler, Richard H., and Shlomo Benartzi. 2004. "Save More Tomorrow: Using Behavioral Economics to Increase Employee Saving." *Journal of Political Economy* 112(S1): S164–S187.

Thaler, Richard H., and H. M. Shefrin. 1981. "An Economic Theory of Self Control." *Journal of Political Economy* 89(2): 392–406.

Thane, Pat. 2000. *Old Age in English History: Past Experiences, Present Issues*. Oxford: Oxford University Press.

Tversky, Amos, and Eldar Shafir. 1992. "Choice under Conflict: The Dynamics of Deferred Decision." *Psychology Science* 3(6): 358–361.

University of Minnesota. *Integrated Public Use Microdata Series*, 1880–2013. Minneapolis, MN.

US Board of Governors of the Federal Reserve System. 1983–2013. *Survey of Consumer Finances*. Washington, DC.

———. 2013a. Selected Interest Rates (Daily)—H.15. Washington, DC. Available at http://www.federalreserve.gov/releases/h15/update/default. htm.

_____. 2013b. *Flow of Funds Accounts of the United States*. Washington, DC.

US Bureau of Labor Statistics. National Compensation Survey, 1999–2012. Washington, DC.

US Census Bureau. 1960. *Historical Statistics of the United States, Colonial Times to 1957*. Washington, DC: Government Printing Office.

US Census Bureau. 1962–2013. *Current Population Survey*. Washington, DC.

US Department of Education. 2011–2012. *National Postsecondary Student Aid Survey*. Washington, DC.

US Department of Housing and Urban Development. 2013. "FHA Reverse Mortgages (HECMs) for Seniors." Available at http://portal.hud.gov/hudportal/HUD?src=/program_offices/housing/sfh/hecm/hecmabou.

US Department of Labor. 1999. *Private Pension Plan Bulletin: Abstract of 1995 Form 5500 Annual Reports*. Washington, DC.

———. 2006. *Annual Return/Report Form 5500 Series for Plan Year 2004*. Washington, DC.

US House of Representatives, Committee on Ways and Means. 2014. "*Tax Reform Act of 2014 Discussion Draft: Section-by-Section Summary.*" Washington, DC.

US Office of Management and Budget. 2013a. *Fiscal Year 2014 Analytical Perspectives: Budget of the U.S. Government*. Washington, DC: Government Printing Office.

———. 2013b. *Fiscal Year 2014 Historical Tables: Budget of the U.S. Government*. Washington, DC: Government Printing Office.

———. 2013c. *Fiscal Year 2014 Budget of the U.S. Government*. Washington, DC: Government Printing Office.

US Senate, Health Education, Labor, and Pensions Committee. 2014. *HELP Chairman Tom Harkin Introduces the USA Retirement Funds Act—Bill Summary*. Washington, DC.

US Social Security Administration. 2004. "Life Table Functions Based on the Alternative 2 Mortality Probabilities in the 2004 Trustees Report." Unpublished.

———. 2013a. "Historical Background and Development of Social Security." Available at http://www.ssa.gov/history/briefhistory3.html.

———. 2013b. *The Annual Report of the Board of Trustees of the Federal Old-Age and Survivors Insurance and Federal Disability Insurance Trust Funds*. Washington, DC: Government Printing Office.

———. 2013c. *Annual Scheduled Benefit Amounts for Retired Workers with Various Pre-retirement Earnings Patterns Based on Intermediate Assumptions, Calendar Years 1940–2090* (Table V.C7). Washington, DC.

———. 2013d. *Principal Demographic Assumptions, Calendar Years 1940–2090* (Table V.A1). Washington, DC.

———. 2013e. "Age 65 Retirement: The German Precedent." Washington, DC. Available at http://www.ssa.gov/history/age65.html.

U.S. Social Security Administration. 2014. *The Annual Report of the Board of Trustees of the Federal Old-Age and Survivors Insurance and Federal Disability Insurance Trust Funds*. Washington, DC: Government Printing Office.

Vanguard. 2013. "*How America Saves 2013: A Report on Vanguard 2012 Defined Contribution Plan Data*." Valley Forge, PA: Vanguard Institutional Investor Group.

———. 2014. "How America Saves 2014: A Report on Vanguard 2013 Defined Contribution Plan Data." Valley Forge, PA: Vanguard Institutional Investor Group.

Venti, Steven F., and David A. Wise. 1989. "Aging, Moving and Housing Wealth." In *The Economics of Aging*, edited by David A. Wise, 9–54. Chicago: University of Chicago Press.

———. 1990. "But They Don't Want to Reduce Housing Equity." In *Issues in the Economics of Aging*, edited by David A. Wise, 13–32. Chicago, IL: University of Chicago Press.

———. 1991. "Aging and the Income Value of Housing Wealth." *Journal of Public Economics* 44(3): 371–397.

———. 2001. "Aging and Housing Equity." In *Innovations for Financing Retirement*, edited by Olivia S. Mitchell, Zvi Bodie, P. Brett Hammond, and Stephen Zeldes, 254–281. Pennsylvania, PA: University of Pennsylvania Press.

———. 2004. "Aging and Housing Equity: Another Look." In *Perspectives on the Economics of Aging*, edited by David A. Wise, 127–180. Chicago: University of Chicago Press.

Waldron, Hilary. 2007. "*Trends in Mortality Differentials and Life Expectancy for Male Social Security—Covered Workers, by Average Relative Earnings*." ORES Working Paper 108. Washington, DC: Social Security Administration.

Weaver, R. Kent. 2004. "Pension Reform in Canada: Lessons for the United States." *Ohio State Law Journal* 65(1): 45–74.

Webb, Anthony, and Natalia A. Zhivan. 2010. "*How Much Is Enough? The Distribution of Lifetime Health Care Costs*." Working Paper 2010-1. Chestnut Hill, MA: Center for Retirement Research at Boston College.

Whitehouse, Edward R., and Asghar Zaidi. 2008. "*Socio-economic Differences in Mortality: Implications for Pensions Policy*." OECD Social, Employment and Migration Working Paper 71. Paris, France: OECD Publishing.

Witte, Edwin E. 1962. *The Development of the Social Security Act*. Madison: University of Wisconsin Press.

Yaari, Menahem E. 1964. "On the Consumer's Lifetime Allocation Process." *International Economics Review* 5(3): 304–317.

INDEX